PRAISE FOR
Healing Grief: A Story of Survivorship

"A single word continued to come to mind as I read this harrowing and ultimately uplifting chronicle of grief and hope - brave, brave, brave! This is a masterful work, a roadmap to post-traumatic growth through the lens of a reluctant and resilient hero."

—Lee Daniel Kravetz, author of SUPERSURVIVORS: The Surprising Link Between Suffering & Success

"This book is so completely human and revealing of emotions most of us don't like to admit that we ever had—and we surely don't expose them. The reader in need of cheer and solace will find Joan a thoughtful and compassionate companion to take on the unplanned and unwanted journey into the Land of the Ill...Such experiences call on us to reach into our depth and find courage, perseverance, even maturity and wisdom that we never suspected we had."

—Jimmie C. Holland, MD, Wayne E. Chapman Chair in Psychiatric Oncology, Memorial Sloan Kettering Cancer Center

"Embedded in this tour de force unfolds a unique, compelling story of vulnerability and strength that has lessons for all those who choose to live a fully conscious life. Miller takes us on a journey of self-exploration that leaves us enriched and inspired."

—Matthew J. Loscalzo, LCSW, Administrative Director, Sheri & Les Biller Patient and Family Resource Center, Liliane Elkins Professor in Supportive Care Programs, Executive Director, Department of Supportive Care Medicine, Professor, Department of Population Sciences, City of Hope National Medical Center

"This book is for healthcare professionals, educators, hospice care professionals as well as anyone touched by significant grief and loss and trauma. Joan's story is especially important for providers in the fields of cancer survivorship, palliative care, and hospice. Each of these specialties struggles to find the balance between the issues of death and dying, and hope and healing. It is essential that healthcare providers pay attention to the psychosocial needs of patients and their families. As I remind my patients, the physical wounds heal quickly; it is typically the psychological wounds that are the hardest to heal. Treating the whole patient, both body and mind, is vital."

—Richard Boyajian, RN, Nurse Practitioner/Clinical Director, Lance Armstrong Foundation Adult Survivorship Program, Dana Farber Cancer Institute

"Joan Miller's memoir recounts her difficult healing journey as a survivor of a terminal illness at a young age, and a subsequent hospitalization for depression. With wisdom and insight, her story gives inspiration and hope to others facing the experience of death and dying. This book will be helpful for professionals in the fields of counseling, social work, medicine, trauma, hospice, and bereavement as well as for the survivors and families facing grief and loss. As the parent of a child who died of a brain tumor, I know how important it is to find exemplars like Joan Miller. She shows how one can cope with adversity, and then go beyond to experience psychological and spiritual growth and transformation. This book is designed to help find the hero in each of us."

—Debbie Schechter, JD, MS, LCPC, Children and Family Grief Support Licensed Counselor and Consultant

"This is a heart-wrenching story of survival and transformation that awaits anyone confronting loss and suffering. An invaluable contribution to the field of psychology, Miller's journey reminds us about the endless possibility of overcoming life's toughest obstacles, and that the opportunity to re-create ourselves and make a new beginning will always remain."

—Suzanne Baer, PhD, Human Development and Aging, Fielding Graduate University

"Joan's emotional journey of near death and despair had me wincing in her pain, but rejoicing as one "grief companion" extended her loving hand for Joan to grasp."

—Susan Jones, author of the award-winning book *Until We Meet Again*

"Miller is a Guardian Angel. She transcends her own loss by dedicating herself to being there for others during difficult periods in their lives."

—James Puska, Connecticut Hospice Bereavement Group Facilitator, and The Cove Center for Grieving Children School Program Outreach Coordinator

Best Wishes & Thanks
for support of
Psycho-Oncology Services
Joan Heller Miller, EdM

Healing Grief

A Story of Survivorship

Joan Heller Miller, EdM

outskirtspress
DENVER, COLORADO

The opinions expressed in this manuscript are solely the opinions of the author and do not represent the opinions or thoughts of the publisher. The author has represented and warranted full ownership and/or legal right to publish all the materials in this book.

Healing Grief
A Story of Survivorship
All Rights Reserved.
Copyright © 2015 Joan Heller Miller, EdM
v3.0

Cover Photo © 2015 Joan Heller Miller, EdM. All rights reserved - used with permission.

This book may not be reproduced, transmitted, or stored in whole or in part by any means, including graphic, electronic, or mechanical without the express written consent of the publisher except in the case of brief quotations embodied in critical articles and reviews.

Outskirts Press, Inc.
http://www.outskirtspress.com

ISBN: 978-1-4787-6001-6

Outskirts Press and the "OP" logo are trademarks belonging to Outskirts Press, Inc.
PRINTED IN THE UNITED STATES OF AMERICA

Table of Contents

Acknowledgments i
The Guest House iii
Foreword v
All Alone 1
Life Before Cancer 6
Cancer 14
Losing Hope 39
Letters to My Grief Companion 50
Lessons Learned Ten Years Out 70
My Experience With the Mental Health System 74
Importance of Finding a Grief Companion 81
Assembling a Coping Toolbox 89
Journaling 91
Heroes and Role Models 94
Mindfulness and Spirituality 96
Humor 99
Post-Traumatic Growth 101
Making Friends With Grief 108
A Special Note from Joan's Psychotherapist 113
Photographs of the Journey 116
References and Resources 125

Acknowledgments

To my special family. Ken, you stayed by my side, which was backbreaking work, and you went to the ends of the earth to keep me alive. I will never be able to thank you enough. Celebrating thirty-five years of marriage is a miracle in so many ways. To our adult children, Cara, Julie, and Jeremy, I am truly blessed to have you in my life. You are each precious, and I'm proud of the exceptional adults you've become.

To each member of our extended families, and to our dear friends who became family at the time, including Adele G., Barbara R., Carin & Paul, Cipie & Dan, David H., Debbie & Howard, Deborah & Ray, Doris & Mark, Elaine & Warren, Elizabeth G., Elizabeth & Alfredo, Ellen & David, Emily T., Emmy & Beth, Glory L., Heidi & Rich, Jackie & Bob, Jane M., Jesse and Davi Fonner, Jody G., Joy R., Karen H., Karen & Arthur, Karen & Tom, Lidia & Milton, Linda & Warren, Marsha R., Mel & Irmgard, Melissa & Eliot, Nancy & Ed, Niti & Prissanna, Paul H., Rob & Ellen, Stephanie W., Sue & Sid, Susie & Mike, and Suzanne B., and to our children's teachers, coaches, and neighbors who took our family under their wings. Your endless greeting cards, calls and visits, healthy meals, babysitting, carpooling, generosity, fundraising for cancer research, infinite support, and unconditional love are gifts our family can never repay.

To my grief companion and psychotherapist, Flora Ingenhousz, LCSW, with gratitude and deep respect. Thank you for your courage to be with me during my times of greatest despair and for your willingness and ability to bear witness to the darkest places of my soul. Your unwavering commitment to trust the process and teach me the same, and to take the journey along with me at each horrible and wonderful step along the way, were the greatest gifts beyond measure.

To the members of my superb medical team, including Walt Alzate, Todd S. Cox, MD, Donna Damico, RN, CNS, Kate Davis, EdD, Roger J. Friedman, MD, Joseph Kaplan, MD, Suzanne Krikawa, RN, Mark J. Levis, MD, Matthew J. Loscalzo, LCSW, Carole B. Miller, MD, Gary K. Palys, MD, Chitra D. Rajagopal, MD, R. Patrick Savage, Jr. PhD, Hedy Schleifer, MA, LMHC, and Yumi Schleifer, PhD, Ronda Schoem, Carol F. Seddon, LCSW-C, BCD, B. Douglas Smith, MD, Elsie L. Turner, MD, Rochelle G. Weinberger, PhD, LCSW, Andrew Winokur, MD, and all others, too many to mention by name, except for you, Felicia, the Snack Lady at the hospital, thank you for keeping me alive.

To my dear colleagues and friends at Hospice Caring, Inc. in Maryland, and The Cove Center for Grieving Children in Connecticut, as well as to the grieving children and families with whom I've had the privilege to work at Mulago Hospital in Kampala, Uganda, and Tikkur Ambassa Hospital in Addis Ababa, Ethiopia, and at schools, camps, and community centers here in the U.S., thank you for being my teachers.

To Cara Miller, PhD, for the beautiful cover design.

A special thanks to Jeremy D. Miller, Jody Franklin, and Justin Alves, RN, for your help shaping this manuscript at different intervals along the way, and to all others for your excellent contributions.

The Guest House

This being human is a guest house.
Every morning a new arrival.

A joy, a depression, a meanness,
some momentary awareness comes
as an unexpected visitor.

Welcome and entertain them all!
Even if they are a crowd of sorrows,
who violently sweep your house
empty of its furniture,
still, treat each guest honorably.
He may be clearing you out
for some new delight.

The dark thought, the shame, the malice,
meet them at the door laughing and invite them in.

Be grateful for whatever comes,
because each has been sent
as a guide from beyond.

> Barks, Coleman. The Essential Rumi: New Expanded Edition.
> New York: Harper Collins Publishers, 2004.

Foreword

IT IS A pleasure to write a foreword for this book that is so completely human and revealing of emotions most of us don't like to admit that we have ever had—and we surely don't expose them. Joan is enormously generous to share the raw feelings associated with facing the threat of death by illness, and threat to psyche by a severe mental depression. She tells the story with grace and dignity by providing excerpts from her diary and then recalls the emotions as a survivor. This "double whammy" illness also occurred at the time of managing young children, a young husband and his career, and her own career aspirations; each is a large task on its own. However, most would agree there is never a "good" time for illness in our lives.

I think the real gift of Joan's book sneaks up on you. By her knowledge and insights, she has provided herself and her experience as the "virtual" grief companion—the one she longed for during illness. The reader in need of cheer and solace will find Joan a thoughtful and compassionate companion to take on the unplanned and unwanted journey into the Land of the Ill. She makes you familiar with the geography of the land with its clinics and hospital rooms, populated by those who often seem to speak another language and care little for the amenities of personhood which are so important for us, wherever we are. How does one get out of this strange place and back into familiar territory of home? Such experiences call on us to reach into our depth and find courage, perseverance, even maturity and wisdom that we never suspected were there. Joan reveals these qualities in this highly personal but also, highly meaningful book. It will serve as a companion for many who are in need.

Jimmie C. Holland, MD
Wayne E. Chapman Chair in Psychiatric Oncology
Memorial Sloan Kettering Cancer Center
New York, NY
June, 2015

All Alone

I LIKE MYSELF bare, skin to the wind, cool breeze blowing through my hair, warm sun shining on my face. These are the joys and privileges I took for granted until they were suddenly stolen away. A masked man lurking in the black of night suddenly steps out from behind a dark alley, frightening me with his crazy eyes. I stop dead in my tracks. There is no place to run to, nowhere to hide. Instantly, without a moment's notice, I have come to the end of the line. Now I must stay and face this nightmare, alone.

Nothing in my Harvard education had prepared me for this. Right now in my memory, I am still alone in my room, sitting on that hard hospital bed, wearing that ridiculous gown. You know, the kind that keeps flying open in the back. Who's the idiot who invented that humiliating thing anyway?

Now, ten months have gone by since my cancer diagnosis and treatments started, and there is still no one in my life who can understand what I went through, or what I'm still going through. I wish I could find a *grief companion*, someone willing to sit by my side, and *not try to change the way I feel*, or make well-meaning, yet, empty promises that I'll definitely get better soon. What I desire most is to have someone simply wrap their arms around my grief and stick by me in these moments of pain.

Although everyone's trying their best, it's hard for the medical staff and my family and friends to bear my tears much longer. They have

◄ HEALING GRIEF

their own problems to deal with, and their own lives to live. People mean well when they try to cheer me up. But when no one will listen to how I am feeling or what I actually went through, it's like living on a different planet than the rest of humanity. If there was just one soul who would simply *be there* to listen, I might begin to feel better again. Floating alone in an atmosphere called Grief is a sad place to be.

Much of what I've endured is too hard to give voice to just yet anyway. It's terrifying to talk about what happened—I may fall apart completely. Or sometimes when I start to cry, I worry that I'll never stop. Yet, if I don't keep trying, I might never feel better or be able to move forward with my life. I'm not sure who I can trust, or if getting my feelings out will actually make things better, not worse.

Writing soothes me. Now, as well as during my initial period of journaling at the hospital, I can take one small step at a time to face what I keep inside. When I put my thoughts on paper, I feel that the weight of my sorrow is lifted, at least for a while. In these pages, I will try to make a place to reveal myself without fear of judgment or shame. Perhaps I'll find relief from the storm, even momentarily. Although I know life will never be the same, maybe this will be a place of comfort and support.

Some say we grow from pain and loss, but for me, all seasons have come to an end. Everything in this garden has died, and I don't know where I'll find the courage to go on. I'll try to keep writing in the hope that one day, this flower will bloom again. As hard as it is to tell my story, I will officially start today. Today is all we know for sure. Tomorrow, for me, might not exist.

Today, I meet you for the very first time. I'm nervous about this business of opening up to a psychotherapist who is a complete stranger, yet, I know I need help, and you seem kind and confident on the phone, so here I am. Ten months have gone by since my cancer diagnosis and treatments, and today is my first counseling session with you. I am so depressed, it feels like I have fallen into a dark cavern where no light penetrates. The doctors label it clinical depression.

ALL ALONE

They've given me different types of medication for depression and anxiety, but they are clearly not working. I hate the side effects—headaches and nausea and weight gain, and now I feel worse than I did before I started taking them.

Though I hardly know if I can trust you yet, I take a grand leap of faith and bring you a part of myself that I have kept hidden. I am testing the waters. Will you react with judgment and ridicule, the very reason I have kept my traumatic experiences close to my chest? Or will you react with empathy and understanding, perhaps even a kind word or two, something to reassure me that I can let go of my burden of inferiority and shame? I imagine that walking over a bed of nails might be easier than disclosing some of the terrifying traumas I endured, so frightening that I can't bring myself to tell anyone the truth about my recent hospital experiences.

You open your office door, and there you stand. Broad smile, eyes shining, arms outstretched. You radiate an inviting presence as if to say, "Welcome, please come in. It would be an honor to know you. Your story is one I'd like to hear. I've been waiting for you, and after such a long journey, now you are finally here." Finding you after two prolonged illnesses, first cancer, and then a deep depression that followed, seems like my first moment of promise.

You ask if I've been sleeping or eating lately, and I confess not much. Then, you ask if I would like a cup of hot tea, a simple gesture that feels profound and makes me feel deeply cared for. Your compassion awakens something from a place deep within me, and I realize this is the first time in a long time that I actually feel any emotion at all. In your offering me such vital sustenance, something shifts inside, as if an invisible flame is rekindled. This spark of light makes me hopeful that my love for the human connection can possibly be restored.

Who knows, maybe I will get better to the point that, one day, I will be able to experience again that simple, yet gratifying feeling that I used to cherish most, which is taking care of another person in need. Feeling emotion again, for the first time in a long time, makes me think I might not be depressed for the rest of my life after all, and this makes me feel better still.

What seems daunting is whether I can trust you, and more importantly, whether spilling out my guts will help me feel better or worse. I've survived my horrifying traumas, but obviously not well, or else I wouldn't be sitting here in your counseling office, would I? Coming right out with the gory details is impossible. Even *contemplating* the idea of telling you my story fills me with dread. Yet, I think to myself, if you care enough to offer me tea as a simple act of kindness, then I will try my best to trust you with my innermost thoughts and feelings.

How honest and open should I be, I wonder? How much am I willing to reveal about what happened during my cancer treatments and that period in my life, and how it affected me psychologically? Do I tell you the *full* truth, or should I tell you maybe *half* the truth? What if you judge me? Or, what if you sit there and think to yourself, "Joan can't really mean that…she can't be telling me what *really* happened!" What if you question the details of my story or doubt I could really be feeling the way I do?

There's something especially comforting about you and being here in your office. Through your window, I can see that the autumn leaves of greens, yellows, and oranges have mostly crumbled and fallen to the ground, but within one pile, I can spot a vivid red maple, my personal favorite, and maybe that's a promising sign. I feel this might be a safe place, and that you may be willing to listen to my story while suspending your own values and judgments. What a gift you would give me by simply being present, while I try to share with you some of most private experiences.

After a good deal of thought, I ask myself, "Hey you, isn't this the whole point of being here? As I try to disclose some deeply personal thoughts and emotions about my experience, I'm respectful of the fact that some of this may be as difficult for you to hear as it is for me to reveal. So, let's take a stab at this together."

What's the very worst thing that could happen, you ask? Well, even if I find the courage to open up, I worry that I might fall apart completely. I'm looking for reassurance. Will sharing my story help me in the long run? How can I really know for sure that something that feels so bad will end up feeling good? I'll never forget the words you said next. "Joan, you're the one in charge. Take one small step at a time. I trust the process of therapy. I know it works. Let's just give this a try?" And so, I begin…

Ten months after being diagnosed with cancer, in the safety of your office, I am able to find the courage to start to tell my story. You make it all right to begin to tell you what happened and how disarmed the incidents made me feel. With no agenda except to be with me where I am at, you listen with compassion, and in turn, I feel heard and validated. What a relief. Turning my former perceptions upside down beginning with today, you give me permission to look at life from a healthier perspective.

Although telling you my story is still scary, as well as embarrassing, it is also healing to divulge the truth. After months of pent-up experiences and emotions being violently tossed about in an ocean of grief, it seems as if a well-worn pearl is beginning to form. Here I've discovered that all things change in time, just like the seasons. It seems that maybe you're the one I can trust.

Born 1958
age 41 in 05/1999

Life Before Cancer

IT WAS ALMOST the year 2000, May of '99, to be exact. I had just turned forty-one and was *on top of life*. I felt truly fulfilled. I had been married to my college sweetheart, Ken, for twenty years. He was in a solo practice as an oncologist and hematologist, a physician specializing in blood disorders and cancer, a tireless profession where he was "on-call" with his patients seven days a week, twenty-four hours a day. He was devoted to his calling and, in my opinion, was and still is one of the smartest, most compassionate physicians you could find. His schedule was so grueling that, at times, I'd confess to friends and family, "In order to get some *real* attention around here, I'd probably need to get cancer."

Meanwhile, I adored being a devoted, hands-on mom for our three young children, ages seven, eleven, and fifteen. Being a "room mother" for all three kids at school, as well as a Girl Scout leader, gave me a great opportunity to use my knowledge in education and child development, counseling and mental health, and my creativity and love for music, drama, and art.

What of my work? I grew up as a young girl always knowing what I wanted to do. I loved all children, especially those who were disadvantaged or had special learning needs, and I knew I wanted to devote my life to teaching and counseling. In the past, I had the privilege of learning from some of the finest teachers in the field of education and counseling, and I was proud at having become a bit of an expert over the past fifteen years on how to help young children, particularly those with special needs, develop language skills through everyday activities and play.

I helped teach deaf and hard of hearing children and teens in public school classrooms, was on the faculty at a local college as an instructor for students working toward their certification in special education, served on the board of local and national organizations, and advocated for educational services for people with hearing loss. This work brought me fulfillment and gave tremendous meaning to my life.

I was also celebrating the birth of my new book, co-authored with a dear friend for life, Sue Schwartz, PhD, called *The New Language of Toys: Teaching Communication Skills to Children with Special Needs*. She and I enjoyed book signing parties and presentations in bookstores, libraries, and schools.

In my spare time, I loved to sing and play guitar, entertain and travel, and I was blessed to have many dear, long-standing friendships. Without a doubt, I was on the move every minute of every day. Oh yes, one more thing to mention. I tried hard to take care of my health, probably drank a bit too much wine, but did what I could to exercise regularly, and tried to stick to low-fat foods.

Although the school year wasn't quite over, the spring flowers in my garden had already begun to bloom in vibrant colors of yellows, purples, and pinks. I noticed feeling run down and especially tired for a few weeks in a row and simply thought to myself, "This too shall pass." Next, I realized that keeping my eyes open became a chore. So I tried to sleep more, began cutting back on my workouts and continued reassuring myself that I was "just overdoing it." I'd heard the expression from family and friends for years. "How do you do everything you do?" I guess my busy lifestyle was just catching up with me. Maybe it was time to re-think my priorities and s-l-o-w down.

After another week, I also began noticing a somewhat unusual, dull, pounding headache which persisted from morning until night, one day after the next. It lingered on, first one week, then the next. Before I knew it, dark black and blue marks mysteriously appeared on

HEALING GRIEF

my legs and arms, and even on my hands, seemingly out of nowhere. There must have been ten of them, or maybe it was more, some as large as two inches in diameter. I wondered what I must keep bumping into. A tiny one appeared on my eyelid, then on my upper lip. In contrast to the sun which shined brightly, my skin started looking more and more pale, and dark circles appeared under my eyes.

Suddenly, breathing became difficult. I'd walk a few steps and would have to stop. I simply could not catch my breath, as if I had just finished swimming a mile. I was aware of this unusual sensation quite often throughout each day, even when awakening after a full night's sleep, drenched in sweat. I even lost five pounds in just a week.

My symptoms started adding up, and my body went from feeling tired and weak to feeling in persistent pain. Strangely, it was as if the sharp aches were coming from deep within the bones themselves. Within a matter of days, the relentless pain radiated to my chest, shoulders and back, until it actually felt like my bones were fracturing apart. It was undeniable. Something was wrong.

Specializing in the diagnosis and treatment of cancer, my husband, Ken, was concerned. He brought me into his office for bloodwork to rule out Coxsackie virus, which I could have contracted from working regularly with young children. When we got the results back, it was that most unusual something in his voice, and that most unusual look in his eyes that gave the truth away. I can look back now and see it was sheer fright, like he had just seen a ghost.

Then I realized he was more than just a little concerned when he quietly announced, "I'm going to take you to the hospital now, just to run a few tests. I think you'd better pack a bag; you may have to stay overnight." I froze in terror. Me? Stay overnight at a hospital? Like most of us who fear one thing or another, I'm no different. Call it a phobia if you will, but mine was that I was terrified of hospitals. I always had been. Odd, given that my husband's work as a cancer physician centered on the busy life of a hospital.

At hospitals, patients walk in through a revolving door that swings one way only, in—but never out. I imagined them in my nightmares as

8

LIFE BEFORE CANCER

housing sick, decrepit remains of men, women, and children whose bodies have started to wither away. I pictured hospitals as desolate places where the sick and dying are sent away from all those who love and care for them. For me, hospitals resembled institutions, and I had always equated them with death.

Stark, isolated rooms on either side of long, dimly-lit hallways, set far away from the rest of humanity, and filled with injured, bloody bodies and acrid smells. Dead quiet except for continuous high-pitched mechanical beeps and groans coming from strange, foreboding machines. Moaning and crying emanating from patient's rooms, people in agony, each one suffering. Hospitals were unbearable and sent shivers up my spine.

When I thought about being sent to a hospital, I thought about being isolated, disconnected from society, adrift, alone. There seemed to be no personal warmth or loving embrace. There was no one there who will know me as the unique human being I was, and instead, I would have to succumb to being "Patient So and So in Room 342." My identity would be gone. Everything that I had poured into my existence to become who I was would disappear.

After an evening of laboratory testing and examinations, I was admitted under the care of a local hematologist-oncologist, a colleague of Ken's. To confirm the anticipated diagnosis and establish a firm treatment plan, I needed to have a bone marrow biopsy, the first of many necessary, yet traumatic medical procedures that confirmed much of what I had always feared about being a hospital patient.

Here's how I described the experience in my journal:

Reluctantly, I get out of Ken's car. He's leaving me at the entrance to the hospital with my suitcase in hand. He promises to come right back after he parks the car. I spot the revolving front door, as well as the lobby through the glass window at the front of the hospital. I don't want to do this. I want to run away. When Ken finds me ten minutes later, I am crouched in the corner of the lobby, hiding from him like

❧ HEALING GRIEF

a child, and hiding from the hell that is awaiting me upstairs on the Cancer Unit.

My heart is racing with fear. Fear of dying, but more urgently, fear of being tortured. It's like a prison chamber up there. No fresh air. Once I go in, there will be no turning back. I have no personal ties here, no one knows me at all. My personal identity will be lost. I'll just be one of hundreds of people just like me, and I'll be treated like a number, not like the individual who I am. My dignity is about to be taken away. There are horrid smells, no hugs or physical warmth, and I'll be at the constant mercy of the hospital doctors and nurses. Please don't make me go up there where no one will care about the person inside this body.

A doctor gave me my first set of orders. "Turn on your stomach… it'll only be uncomfortable for a minute." I watched out the corner of my eye as the technician secretly produced a thick, six-inch hypodermic needle and horse-size syringe from behind his back, and with one fell swoop, inserted it into my lower hip as far as it would go, pulling out actual marrow from deep inside the bone. I could feel my breath being drawn out, right along with the contents of his syringe. I screamed louder than I knew was possible. So this is how it must feel to have a butcher knife stabbed in your back. *Never, ever say the word uncomfortable again.* I was furious! I had also just discovered what I feared about hospitals the most…hospital personnel didn't always tell the truth.

Over the next twenty-four hours, I had to have my blood drawn close to a dozen times to see if I would need transfusions. That's equivalent to twelve annual flu shots, all in one day. But, in comparison to the bone marrow biopsy, getting all those sharp needles was a piece of cake.

Later that same morning, my oncologist walked into the room, and with a serious expression explained, "We finally figured out why you are so sick. The tests have all confirmed you have AML." By then, I had been feeling rotten for so many months that when a doctor finally

LIFE BEFORE CANCER

came up with a diagnosis, I was actually relieved. AML. Hmmm. I'm not entirely sure what that is—maybe a virus of some kind? Well, at least now the doctors can figure out how to make me better. You'd think being married to an oncologist, I would have had some knowledge about what AML was, but frankly, I hadn't recalled hearing that abbreviation before.

Once the doctor left, a kind nurse came into my room soon thereafter. She sat at the foot of my bed and gently asked if I understood what the doctor had just told me. "You have AML, acute myelogenous leukemia, a fast-growing blood cancer." I listened in shock to her words. "The prognosis for this type of leukemia is not the best, but you have a real shot at making it because you're young, and otherwise in good health. Any chance of survival will mean a long road ahead. You will need intensive treatment, which will require that you sleep here at the hospital for the next five weeks in a row, and then come back four more times over the next six months. Between each cycle, you can go home and get daily treatments as an outpatient, which will help your body replenish its resources between each inpatient cycle. Fortunately, we are one of the leading hospitals for treating your type of illness. You'll need to be admitted immediately."

The next words I heard her say made me sob uncontrollably. "If you make it through your treatments without too many difficult complications, you have a twenty or twenty-five percent chance of survival over the next five years." What I heard her say was that I would die in five years, even if I was lucky enough to make it through my treatments.

Once the nurse told me what my chances were, I immediately thought, "Oh-my-God. I-am-going-to-die!" Cancer cells had spread throughout my bloodstream, robbing oxygen from every cell. Now I finally understood why my peculiar symptoms of ongoing pain were ones like I had never experienced before. *That's* why I had had an impossible time breathing, *that's* why I had lost weight, had been so weak and fatigued, and in such unmanageable pain.

I had been dying already for so many weeks, and I would die

soon, maybe even within a week or two, if I didn't start treatments immediately. Any chance of survival though, meant having to stay there and face what I feared the most. Learning the grim news that death was approaching felt as if a brick building had collapsed on my head, or as if I had just been handed down a death sentence——"You have cancer, a terminal illness." *Terminal.* I knew what that meant. That meant *deadly*. Last week, I was alive. Next week, I could be dead.

It felt as if ice water was being poured through my veins. My body froze in terror. Like a deer realizing it is stuck in the cross-hairs of a hunter's gun, at that moment, my heart stopped. I felt that I, too, was about to die. I heard myself scream, "I'm going to die!" There's no escape. My head dropped into my hands as I sobbed like never before, my body racked with fear. I was inconsolable. I heard the nurse quietly excuse herself to give me some time alone. At that precise moment, I learned the true meaning of the word *time* in a way I thought I knew, but never fully understood before. Now, each moment could truly be my last. Each moment counted, like never before.

Ken had just left moments before with the three kids. He had brought them to the hospital as soon they got home from school on that fateful day. The kids cried and hugged me, wanting to hold on extra tight, when we shared the news that I had cancer and would need to stay there at the hospital in order to get better. They were sad and scared and, of course, so were Ken and I.

Now I was all alone. I reached for the phone on my bedside table and frantically dialed the first number I could think of, one of my best friends. Thankfully, she answered. I wailed into the phone, "I'm scared! I'm going to die!" She said back, "What's wrong? What's happened? Try to catch your breath so you can speak!" Between sobs, I told her I was at the hospital. "Which one? I'll get in the car right now," she promised. "Where's Ken? Do you need me to reach him for you?" I told her that he and the kids had just left. She said she would get a hold of him immediately, and after calling his cell phone again and again, she couldn't begin to imagine why he didn't pick up.

There was a reason why. As Ken began the one-hour drive home

LIFE BEFORE CANCER

with our three children on the interstate highway, a real deer became stuck in the headlights. In sheer panic and desperation, it leapt across two lanes of the interstate and crashed into the car's windshield. Ken smacked his chin against the steering wheel and glass went flying into the car. Ken managed to steer the car to safety into the emergency lane as the children were screaming and crying. "First Mom has cancer. Now *this!*"

Just a half an hour before, the kids were terrified to learn that Mom could die from cancer, and now, their own lives flashed before them. In the blink of an eye, the world had become an unpredictable, unsafe place.

Cancer

I HAVE *CANCER*. The words spun through my brain. And death was approaching fast. There was no time to waste. In a matter of moments, the life I knew and loved would vanish. I knew the worst of this, because cancer had invaded our lives for well over twenty years; my husband was an oncologist, after all. Death had wormed its way into each public and private corner of our lives. Countless stories of struggle, some promising, others not, were shared at the family dinner table, or during intermission at our daughters' theater or dance performances, or during half-times at their school basketball games.

Ken and I were often awakened in the middle of the night by phone calls from hospital nurses, diligently requesting "doctor's orders" for sleeping pills, stool softeners, but mostly for meds to ease their patients' pain. The shrill ringing of the pager, announcing death, was the musical backdrop to our lovemaking, sometimes even defeating moments of blissful orgasm. When death comes, it takes over all of life. The actual physician report was shocking:

"Mrs. Miller, a pleasant forty-one year old woman has been diagnosed with high-grade Myelodysplastic Syndrome. She has an advanced case with a white blood count of 40,000 with a 24% blast count in the peripheral blood and 18% blasts in the bone marrow. The bone marrow is markedly hypocellular and is packed with immature cells on the biopsy. Megakaryocytes range from hypolobulated to fully lobulated. Also, there are hypogranulated and abnormal metamyelocytes and hypogranulated promyelocytes noted. The only

CANCER

therapy with a curative intent is a bone marrow transplant. An unrelated donor transplant carries a higher morbidity and mortality; however, there is data that suggesting that an allo-transplant may be curative. We need to activate a search as soon as possible given the aggressive nature of her disease."

In my journal that evening, I wrote:

I know no one who has ever had Acute Myelogenous Leukemia. Either that, or they didn't live long enough to tell me about it. Yes! That must be the precise reason why I've never heard of it before. How am I going to get through this? How will I be tough enough to handle this? Forget it! I am the wrong person for this job.

I am scared to death. Oh no, I better not use that expression ever again! I can't do this. I'm just not strong enough! What does dying feel like? Will I die in pain? How much pain? Will it feel something like a rocket, my life force hurling into space with no other mission than to explode on impact? There is no turning back the hands of time. No way out of this mess. I feel helpless. What is left to do, except brace for death? I never felt each final moment before now. I've never felt life coming to an end.

It's not fair! This is not the time to die! I'm not ninety, or eighty, or seventy. That's when a person's supposed to die. I just turned forty-one, at the pinnacle of life! I haven't even hit the big 5-0! I'll only have the privilege of experiencing forty-one years. Forty-one years and my life will be cut short. Forty-one years with no warning, and no time left to say goodbye. Although life will continue on for all those around me, mine will abruptly end.

And what about Ken and our three children, and our parents, brothers, aunts, uncles, cousins, and the whole rest of our family and friends I love so much, all who will have to go on without me? I am just a young mom, with three little girls. They haven't reached high school yet, let alone college. Our three little girls will have to grow up without me, maybe even without a mother at all during their formative

◂ **HEALING GRIEF**

years. Who's going to teach them about getting their first menstrual period, or assist them when it's time to fill out their college applications, or help them out with child care when the grandchildren arrive?

Ken will be all alone, without his partner and friend of twenty-five years. I helped write his college papers and study for his exams, surprised him with banners and balloons when we celebrated the good news that he was accepted into medical school, helped him to build his medical practice, and kept him organized and on-track. What will he do without me?

Our parents will be crushed to lose a child, for my parents especially, their only daughter. Having to witness their child endure such debilitating treatments over the next six months or more will be agonizing for them. Just a moment ago, I could see my entire life stretched out in front of me, and now, just one moment later, my life is gone! All the pleasures I know, and all that brings me joy, especially the people I love, will disappear at the snap of a finger, just like that. I am dying now.

It was naive of me to believe all these years that the universe was ordered in any sort of predictable or sensible way. First you're born, then you grow up, then you go to college, you get a job, you get married, have kids, travel, have grandkids, enjoy your senior years—and then die, only after having lived a full, rich life.

Maybe my death was part of a larger wicked scheme of some sort? Perhaps there was some good reason why my number was up. But what could I have possibly done that was so wrong that I should deserve this? Was I being punished now for those rebellious teenage years spent lying in the sun, slathered in coconut oil? Or could it be that Ken unknowingly brought home a live cancer virus from the hospital laboratory?

Up until that very moment, I never believed in God. But now, suddenly, I did. At first, I just kept praying, "Please don't let me die. Please don't let me die." It was automatic, like a voice that took over inside me. "I'm sorry I never believed in you before. I'm so, so sorry.

◂ 16

CANCER

Please forgive me. Promise you won't punish my family and friends and me this way. I'll change my ways. I'll do it right now." I continued bargaining, "Dear God, I'll do anything, anything at all, if you'll just let me live, and I'll never ask for anything again."

I hadn't sinned—well, not much. Though, there was that one time I had stolen candy from that gift shop where I worked when I was fourteen. But, what other trouble had I caused, or what else could I think of that would make God this angry at me? Perhaps this explained the guilt I'd been carrying for all these years, convinced I had somehow caused our daughter's deafness. Maybe there *was* something I had done, without even realizing it. My past was finally catching up with me. This must be the reason I was chosen to die at such a young age.

It's almost impossible to explain the fright of complete powerlessness except to imagine an impending natural disaster—a tsunami swallowing everyone in its path, or an earthquake, or hurricane, or a fire racing to the top of a twenty-story building where you're stranded, knowing you're about to become engulfed in flames.

Departures were not my strong suit. In fact, I was just plain lousy with goodbyes. Ask my husband; I always had been. I have an enormous case of separation anxiety. I'll admit it. Take my first day of preschool. It was a nightmare. Hard to believe, but I can still recount the terrifying experience of saying goodbye to my mother on that first day of school, being left behind in that giant brick building, when I was just not ready. When I close my eyes, I can still conjure up that terrifying vision of my mother pulling away and leaving me behind, feeling scared and alone. My tiny, three-year-old voice bellowed, "Mommy, don't leave me!" I can still feel my tightly clenched hand pulling at the hem of her skirt as she tried to head out the door. So, imagine what it was like for me, now that I'd be apart from all those I love for good. This time, I needed to bid farewell once and for all.

The doctor explained that my inpatient treatment would require intravenous chemotherapy, twenty-four hours around the clock. In the back of my mind, I was sure chemotherapy drugs were poisonous, designed to kill. I just couldn't shake the petrifying mental image of

◄ HEALING GRIEF

Hitler, the mad man who designed the most devious, cruel ways of torturing human beings, as he schemed to wipe out an entire race of innocent, kind people. He had masterminded an evil way to torment his victims using a deadly concoction of chemicals, infusing them into helpless human beings, who would then die a slow, agonizing death. Within minutes, his victims would gasp for air, harder and harder, until their lungs were ready to burst.

I could not imagine a torture greater than this, and I was next in line. I simply could not erase such visions of concentration camps and tortured sad souls, marching into the gas chambers. Hollow cheeks, skin and bones, eyes staring blankly into space, shaved, bald heads, stringy hair, and lifeless forms marching off to death. Next, I would become the innocent victim who was being torn from my family, friends, and my community, cut off from the human race. In my case, that's what finding out I had cancer felt like.

Until then, I suppose I had a foolish sense that everything works out, all in due time. Tragedies only happen to *other* people, like the ones you read about in newspapers or watch on the TV news. Not this time—this tragedy was *mine*. My frame of reference instantly shifted from *Life is good* to *Life is a nightmare!* I continued to perseverate, "Where will I go after I die? Heaven? Or Hell! Will I be met by angels, or fire and brimstone?"

As a cancer patient, I would no longer be in charge of making decisions. In the blink of an eye, I would become a puppet. Someone else entirely will pull my strings. Immobilized, I wouldn't be able to take one step forward, sideways, or back. There was nothing I could do, nowhere to hide. I knew the facts. Once admitted to the hospital, patients lose control, and subject themselves to unyielding demands made by the "medical team." It's in the patients' best interest. I understood that.

Any sense of self-determination or freedom of choice would be gone. My ability to make even the most basic decisions, such as what to eat and when, which we take for granted, would be suddenly stolen away. I would lose any sense of control over my life. In turn, life for me, would feel out of control. Powerful figures in our medical hierarchy would dictate how I would spend each last moment on this earth.

For hospital patients, there are strict rules that must be followed. Order and discipline is expected. Patients do precisely what they are told, because their lives are at stake. Taking orders is part and parcel of the fact that we are at the mercy of a larger system called the American Medical Bureaucracy.

One of the first orders the doctor wrote in my medical chart was that I would not be allowed to eat. I would only be permitted to get "nutrition supplements" through an IV catheter during the first, five-week inpatient treatment cycle. This decision, he explained, was made in an effort to prevent serious "gastrointestinal side effects." Although I understood the reason from a medical advantage, tears welled up in my eyes.

I knew I needed to change my perspective from feeling like a victim to feeling empowered, like a soldier marching off to war. With Ken's help and support, my only chance at getting through this was to try to develop a different attitude altogether. "You can beat this," he declared. And then he said the sweetest and most loving words I ever heard him say to me before. "I will take this journey with you step by step. We'll do this together." His words made my heart melt, because they overflowed with the depth of his love. "For better or worse," he said with great tenderness and compassion. My mind raced back to our marriage ceremony twenty years earlier. These were the same words he had promised me as we stood together, holding hands and gazing into each other's eyes during our wedding ceremony. Hold on...was he now trying to tell me that the journey we were about to take would be the "worse" referred to in those vows?

Ken suggested I practice replacing any and all frightening images with powerful, positive ones of chemotherapy drugs battling the bad cells until only the healthy ones remained. "You'll keep on fighting until you eradicate every one of those cancerous cells, and I'm going to do this with you. We'll do this together, one step at a time."

HEALING GRIEF

As my anxiety climbed, I spent hours perfecting my skills in visualization, imagining a vivid sunrise, or a sailboat gently moving across the water. I consulted with a friend who was an expert in pain management techniques, pulled books off my shelf on how heroes maintain a positive attitude in the face of adversity, and I explored additional literature on survival techniques which I thought might help. Remembering my mantra from that class I took in college twenty years before, "Ahhh, eeem...Ahhh, eeem...," I practiced deep breathing and meditation all over again.

But above everything, I told myself I had to do what it takes. Realizing I had no choice, I'd simply have to close my eyes, put one foot in front of the other, and repeat to myself again and again, "Joan, you can do this...Joan, you can do this!" just like the story of *The Little Engine That Could,* one of my favorite childhood classics. I'd try my best to suppress those ghastly visions of Nazi victims and replace them instead with images of radar guns zapping away my bad cancer cells. Developing a new attitude would mean taking on a different approach, lightening up if I could, and trying to develop a sense of humor. Anything was worth a try.

Here's what I wrote in my journal at the end of that first day:

Having to say goodbye to life is greater than any loss I could have imagined, or any pain I have ever known. Previous notions of time and predictability have suddenly vanished, like a magician's black cape, twirled around to reveal in an instant, Nothing. I have been meditating on the meaning of time. My days are now measured in moments, each one savored more than ever, like reaching to the bottom of the mixing bowl, savoring that last bit of cookie dough, down to the very last drop. Think of how much we depend on time to measure our existence: Instant coffee. There's no time like the present. Time is money. Not a moment too soon. Better late than never. Life can turn on a dime. Not a moment to waste.

Time s-l-o-w-s down, each sound and sight becoming more

pronounced, each heartbeat pounding louder than before. The pendulum swinging on a grandfather clock, ticking slower and slower and slower still. These are the winding down of minutes as you near your final end. Beyond that moment, there would be no more, not even one. Each grain of sand in the hourglass has run out. Time is at an end. I feel completely alone, like a prisoner, as if being hauled away from all of humanity and locked up in solitary confinement forever and always.

When a person gets sick and goes to a doctor, it's normal to ask, "How many days before I'll feel better? How many days until I get back to my old self?" For me, this question no longer exists. The question is no longer how many days before I get better, but how many more days do I have left to live?

Leukemia was an unexpected, but vital "appointment" to add to my already bulging "To Do List." I reached into my purse and fumbled to pull out my blue vinyl day-timer to study what manner of inconvenience this sudden death sentence would cause. So many back-to-back appointments and responsibilities centered around the life of my three young children, my husband's, and my own. I couldn't possibly get ready to go into the hospital early the next morning, let alone get ready to sleep there for the next five weeks.

It said right there in my day-timer that I was expecting twelve people for dinner the following Friday night, and I had been shopping, cooking and baking for a solid week already. It felt impolite to call friends at the last minute, asking them to reschedule social plans whenever something came up on my end. I looked at what was written down for the week after that one. I had a dentist appointment that Wednesday at 2:00 pm which I had to schedule six months in advance. I couldn't possibly miss that either. It might take another month or more to wait for a cancellation. My eyes kept scanning the weekly appointments penciled in blue, red, black, purple, or orange color-coded marks scrawled across each page. I looked at all these other important things I needed to get done on my "Must Do List."

I had no time to have cancer. I reached for a pen, and hesitantly, I wrote in bold, diagonal script across the next five weeks in my calendar, "SLEEP AT THE HOSPITAL. INPATIENT TREATMENTS." Then, I realized the comic relief. I could finally do the very thing I had wished for during the past twenty years—throw my damn day-timer away altogether! All these other appointments would just have to wait until after I found out if I was going to live or not. Miraculous how all my previous vital appointments were not so urgent after all.

Instead of a day-timer, I needed heroes to rely on. Some of the world's most courageous people throughout history flashed through my brain. Now I needed to join their ranks, lean on their success, and emulate them as pillars of fortitude. "Joan, you must be like them now; if they can do it, you can too." I reassured myself that I had what it took to tackle the road that lay ahead. I made up my mind that no matter what, I would stay mentally focused on my goal to fight my cancer. I would learn all that I could from others facing cancer, as well as from healthcare professionals about how to survive the harrowing treatments that lie ahead. Soon after my diagnosis, a well-meaning cancer survivor approached me and said, "You'll see, cancer will change your life for the better." However, I didn't believe him. I knew that his platitude was only meant to make me feel better.

To maximize my chances for survival, no matter how slim, I'd have to persevere, not just for myself, but for Ken and our three young children, our parents, brothers, sisters, extended family and friends. People had commented that in the past, I'd been a model of strength for family and friends, and now, I would simply have to do it again. I would make people proud of me, and show by example that no matter what, I wouldn't let them down.

My unbelievably helpful family and friends stepped up their commitment even more, something which was impossible to imagine. In fact, my illness brought out the most reverent love and compassion in most every person whose life I had touched. Word spread like wildfire through the community that I had been diagnosed with a life-threatening illness. There was a tremendous outpouring of generosity and expression of caring and concern that erupted like nothing I had ever witnessed before. Friends and neighbors climbed on board to do all that they could to help my family survive. Prayer groups were organized up and down the Eastern seaboard, organized by ministers and rabbis who spread the word about my dire health. Complete strangers prayed for my survival, for heaven's sake. How's that for love and conviction of the human spirit?

Our family's neighborhood swim team with close to seventy-five families mobilized forces, making sure our family was fed a delicious meal each night for the first five weeks I'd be spending at the hospital. My husband and children never had it so good! Soon thereafter, the local parent-teacher organization with which I'd been affiliated as a board member and volunteer for fifteen years, with more than three hundred and fifty families, teachers, and administrators working together as advocates for children with special needs, also climbed on board to make meals for my family for the next six months. First there was chicken. Then there was more chicken. Next, there was lasagna. Then, there was more lasagna. When good friends appeared with filet mignon, insisting it would help my red blood cells, we were speechless.

Loving, compassionate friends and family, as well as kind neighbors, took on duties of parenting and other responsibilities at home or work. People could simply not do enough to help, and the plan they developed for the coordinated care of our family worked seamlessly. What was left for me to do but to contribute my share to the team? I could be a tough soldier, and I promised to come back stronger than before.

Recalling the collective voices of family and friends who insisted I had overcome more obstacles than most anyone they'd known, I tried convincing myself I could succeed again. After all, who doesn't like hearing from their cheering squad of family and friends, "You are amazing! You will get through this, just like all the other obstacles you've overcome." Encouraging friends, family, and colleagues empowered me to face my treatments and to "give it my best shot."

HEALING GRIEF

I shaved off my gorgeous, long hair before my first round of chemotherapy treatments, in order to spare myself and others the shock of what I would look like when my own hair fell out in a week or two as a result of the high levels of chemotherapy. Another idea I came up with was to fool around with our family, including my father and brothers, and try on an assortment of wigs in different colors and styles loaned to us from our local hospital's Cancer Hope Chest. I enthusiastically asked, "Hey everyone, want to have some fun?"

Our youngest one looked precious in a brunette curly wig, just like Annie, straight out of the movie. To our oldest child, who had just turned fifteen, all we could say was, "Who knew you'd look so great as a redhead?" And we all admired the platinum blond number that our middle daughter picked out. "It makes you look simply ravishing, Dahl-ing!" Even our golden retriever, Caramel, got in the action. When she sported a senior citizen, pure gray number, the rest of us couldn't stop laughing.

I kept on the lookout for additional strategies I could come up with to help me get through my upcoming, "Round One," the first of four, five-week cycles of inpatient treatments I would need to help cure my cancer, and to stay motivated throughout the process.

We all know that some people are better with pain than others. My tolerance is on the low side, shall we say. I'm the type of person who gets a paper cut, then whines like a puppy with a thorn stuck in its paw. A sprained ankle might keep me laid up for weeks. To build up my courage to face what lay ahead, I tried to recount each one of the most difficult experiences I had ever mastered to help build my confidence and confirm my conviction that I could get through this ordeal, too.

Take, for example, my first experience with childbirth. At that time, I was young and pretty scared to begin with. There was something about the whole idea of building a tall ship inside a small bottle, then having to get it out. As luck would have it, delivering our first child turned out to be a medical crisis, when during the last few hours of labor, the doctor unexpectedly discovered the baby was breech.

CANCER

Moreover, it was what's called a transverse breech, one of the highest risk types of delivery. The baby's hard bottom came out first, with her legs and feet crossed, as if in a yoga stance, her head positioned last. I was in the very last stage of hard labor, when gripping contractions were multiplying by the minute. There was no time for anesthesia, no time for an epidural, no time for an episiotomy, not even two Tylenol. I can still hear the doctor persistently begging me to "stop screaming" until I heroically pushed her out. It was well worth it. When her sweet little face emerged at the final end, I cried with joy and relief.

Then there was the grief of finding out the shocking news that our baby was born deaf and struggling with the shattered dream of bringing into the world a perfect baby with ten perfect fingers and ten perfect toes. Life's toughest obstacles also meant facing the disappointment and worry the news would bring to our parents, all four of them waiting a lifetime to finally welcome their first granddaughter into their lives. Would she ever learn to talk? Would she be able to go to a "regular school"? Who would want to be her friend? Would she get a job? Get married? Our lives would never be the same.

When life gives you lemons, make lemonade. That was the credo I tried to live by. Giving birth to a baby who was profoundly deaf was such an example. The possibility of one day transforming that loss and grief into something greater was inspiring. I was proud that I could give her the same level of education and possibility as any child with hearing. The fact that I had transformed my own grief into something positive gave my life purpose and meaning. Fifteen years later, raising a child who was deaf had gone from a seemingly impossible task, to a welcome challenge, and then a gift beyond measure.

Nevertheless, I was still worried about how I'd ever be able to get through my treatments. I had said for years that if women knew how much childbirth hurt, they wouldn't get pregnant at all. I was now certain this rule applied to patients with advanced cancer battling their grueling treatments. If anyone had sat me down beforehand to explain in detail the harrowing treatments required, as well as the expected side effects of the treatments or problems that might otherwise arise, I would have flat-out refused any treatment at all.

If only someone could have removed my brain, and then put it back when the treatments were over, maybe I would have done better. I would try to maintain that same, tough spirit I had needed to call on in the past. But by the third five-week-long inpatient visit, my motto had shifted from taking small, manageable steps one day at a time to one moment at a time.

Upon awakening after my first night at the hospital, I was wheeled down to the operating room. I use the word *awakening* loosely for I'm sure I didn't sleep for a minute that first night. Unlike that first invasive bone marrow procedure, the next procedure I needed was done under general anesthesia, thank goodness! It required feeding an in-dwelling catheter, about ten inches long, deep into my chest wall, close to my clavicle, just below the neck. At this particularly vulnerable juncture, chemotherapy drugs, new red blood cells and platelets, and pain medications such as Demerol and morphine were filtered directly into the vena cava, the largest vein in the body. Next, a second plastic line, this one, five feet in length, was attached from the catheter, which was embedded in my chest, to a portable intravenous pump on wheels, valiantly named the IVAC, on which was hanging several bags of medicines that were keeping me alive. The challenge was to manage keeping my body attached to this "five-foot-tall lifesaving device" seven days a week, twenty-four hours a day. "It can follow you wherever you go," I was reassured by the nurses. It followed me into the bathroom when I had to pee, or over to the sink nearby my bed when I needed to frequently vomit from the chemotherapy drugs. It followed me down the hall when I forced myself to try to take a walk, despite my fatigue, or even in the elevator for trips to the MRI or X-ray departments.

There was no escape from the ambient mechanical sound that signaled when a bag became empty and needed to be replaced immediately, or if a line was twisted or kinked. If I accidentally moved one step too far, either to the left, or to the right, too far forward, or too far back, the long, sturdy line attached to my IV pole yanked hard at the stitches at my sore incision site on my neck which was already hot to the touch, and swollen and painful, even without this additional insult. The experience of being limited in motion day and night while being tethered to a metal pole felt somewhat degrading. At times, I wondered if this was how a dog must feel each time his master pulls hard on the leash. Unlike a beloved canine, not for a moment did I feel like man's best friend.

Nothing could have prepared me for the incident with the IVAC that happened soon after I was admitted. It was in the middle of the night. As I lay sleeping, no one was paying attention to safely monitor the steady flow of IV fluids that were being pumped into my veins by the IVAC. At a critical juncture where the plastic tubing must stay tightly connected and in a locked position, the connection became unscrewed ever so slowly, until the two ends detached completely.

While I lay sleeping on my back, over several unmonitored hours while the nurse was attending to other severely ill patients, my blood began to silently leak out of the plastic tubing that had unscrewed, drop by drop, until my mattress was so absorbed with blood that it was completely soaked. Thick, dark blood coated the back of my head and shoulders, my buttocks, calves and heels as I lay quietly sleeping, sedated from high doses of morphine for bone pain. At that point, the night-shift nurse and I were completely unaware that the tubing needed to be re-attached immediately.

My blood continued to seep out, first dripping onto the floor from the left side of my bloody soaked mattress, and then dripping onto the floor form the right. Finally, I was lulled awake from my deeply medicated sleep. What was that faint, unfamiliar smell, something with an unpleasant metallic odor?

Like a newborn doe, my ears quickly perked up. The unfamiliar dripping sound and smell alerted me to danger. My senses began to sharpen. Was it beginning to drizzle outside? Perhaps what I was hearing was the gentle rain pelting against my window pain, or maybe it was a steady drip coming through from a tiny crack in my ceiling. I listened harder. In the dim light of my room, I looked around some more, intent on finding the source. Something was definitely wrong. There was definitely something dripping, and I was certain that the sound was coming from underneath my bed. Yet, how could that be? I suddenly realized where the sound was coming from. It was my blood splattering like rain onto the floor.

In my drugged stupor, I managed to hunt for my emergency call button. Instructing my hand to work somehow, I pressed it. One nurse appeared at my door in a matter of moments. I watched her jaw silently drop open as soon as she immediately assessed the near fatal situation. She was taken aback. Gazing at the puddles of blood on the floor below my bed, and hearing that faint but steady, drip, drip, drip of my blood, then noticing my sheer white face, she instantly figured out what had happened. She could tell I was fading fast.

The nurse dashed out and summoned in two more. Three in white surrounded me, their hands and arms moving quickly, every which way, rotating my body to mop off the blood that had already begun to coagulate and harden, while at the same time, trying desperately to strap an oxygen mask over my nose and mouth to force air into my lungs. They panicked, and so did I, that I had lost too much blood and I was dying.

Caught in a dilemma, I did not want to tell the head nurse that the oncology nurses were neglectful and had allowed such a potentially deadly error to occur. The nursing staff would be severely disciplined, and I was sure they'd be furious with me. Afraid they might get in trouble or even lose their jobs as a result of this grave mistake, I decided to keep this traumatic incident to myself.

The oncology nurses on the front line of duty were the ones whose job it was to keep a steady eye on me. Dependent on them for their tender care and soothing touch, I could not afford to make them angry, for I was worried they might handle my sore body in a rough or forceful manner. It was their caring attention and hopeful words that kept me going. I decided at that time to keep this incident to myself, and so, this dark secret about the nurses' human error that almost caused my death remained ours alone. I trusted from that point on that the nurses on duty would be extra vigilant. They would *definitely* make sure a mistake like that would never happen again.

Lo and behold, lightning struck twice. Around midnight six nights later, I began to sense an all-too-familiar smell and sound. As I tuned in more carefully, I deciphered that same metallic odor. Immediately leaning over my bed, I once again watched in disbelief and horror as my blood slowly dripped out of that same plastic tube juncture that had unscrewed yet again.

Death closed in, luring me to surrender. My thoughts became jumbled and disjointed, and I felt myself fading away. My breath grew shallow and quiet, like the calm breathing of a newborn baby. Feeling my body lift toward the sky, it felt light and buoyant, like a hot air balloon gently drifting upward. It is hard to describe, and I'm sure even more difficult to believe, but it seemed as if my soul was searching for a new life form to enter. It didn't seem like I was dying as much as it felt like my spirit was floating onward. I felt that now I understood! So *this* is what it would feel like to die. Once again, the medical staff quickly surrounded me, and, with an oxygen mask clasped to my face, guided me back to life.

In this scenario, I was grateful for the medical intervention that saved my life. However, in most cases, life in the hospital presented challenges to my most basic freedoms. Days were organized around adults commanding me exactly when to do things and just what to do. Maintaining this level of obedience made me feel helpless, and that I was at the mercy of the doctors, nurses, and lab technicians at all times. Hospital rules were clearly spelled out, all of which I was expected to follow. Being awakened from a sound sleep at midnight to be wheeled down in the elevator for an MRI test my doctor had ordered earlier that morning, to rule out bleeding into the brain, was annoying. Most times, there is hardly any sense of day or night in an oncology unit; there are so many patients with life-threatening illnesses that important medical tests are scheduled around the clock.

Some hospital rules were completely understandable. Others

were not just frustrating, they were humiliating and demeaning, especially given the fact that I was desperately weak and in pain. There was little reserve left to maintain a sense of humor, or to push past the pain. The first five-week inpatient stay was very hard, especially because I was not allowed to eat solid food. But I still tried to keep a stiff upper lip and stick with the program as best I could. But as the weeks passed on, and certainly by the end of that first month in the hospital, being forced to obey annoying rules became outright infuriating.

As an example, a nurse came into my room while I was asleep one night, and flicked on the bright fluorescent light above my hospital bed, with a resounding, "Time for your sleeping pill!" You've got to be kidding, I cried. Why do you need to wake me up at two o'clock in the morning just to give me a sleeping pill when *I'm already asleep!* "These are the doctor's orders!" the cheerful, yet compliant nurse replied. "But I *don't need* a sleeping pill!" "I'm sorry," the nurse replied, "but to change that order, I'll have to check with the doctor first to make sure he would give his medical consent. Because the doctor's making rounds in the hospital right now and has many more patients to see, it's likely I won't be able to reach him for a while. Why don't you just take the pill anyway since I'm here right now?" I felt weak and in physical pain, and experiences like these made me feel emotionally and mentally drained as well.

Another rule that was degrading as well as disgusting was being required to collect and save all of my urine and feces throughout the day. "Are you serious? Do I *really* have to do that?" The nursing staff insisted this collection was for medical reasons, to calculate and measure what was going in and what was going out, and being the ever obedient patient, I cringed, but complied.

Sometimes, however, an entire seven-hour nursing shift would go by without someone from the staff taking responsibility for following up on this obnoxious rule. Humiliated, I'd ring the nurse's call button to ask if someone would hurry and come into my room, measure my excrement, then discard the damn stuff! By the time the next nursing shift rolled around, I began to lose my eternal patience. "I hate to ask you this for the second time, but would you *please empty out* the contents of my toilet? It smells *terrible* in here." On more than one occasion, a nurse would respond with the comment, "Hmm...I think I may have to ask *someone else* to stop by later to take care of that."

Once I began the intensive chemotherapy which was required for any chance of survival, the initial things that I feared began to happen all at once. As I gazed hesitatingly into the mirror, I recognized that the harrowing image of that bald and sad looking cancer patient was mine. As someone who had always taken great pride in her appearance, it was hard to look at myself. I looked hideous, felt humiliated, and was convinced that others saw me this way as well. Although it may have been unusual for other cancer patients, I did not want friends to come around because I looked and felt so downright miserable.

People associate chemotherapy with constant vomiting and that dreadful sensation of sickening nausea. For some cancer patients this is one of the most grueling parts of their treatment, but fortunately for me, it was often manageable. Medical researchers and physicians have come up with effective medications that reduce nausea and vomiting to a tolerable level, and for this, I was thankful.

One morning, in particular, was going along pretty well. My pain was under control, since mornings, for me, were the best time of day for pain management. A nurse walked into my room to hang a chemotherapy bag on my IV pole. Our eyes were glued to the tiny television screen in the far corner or my room. Lance Armstrong's race came on the set and his determination to win, once again, helped motivate me to face my own course. If Lance could do it, so could I. The nurse was not paying attention to her job of properly administering the chemotherapy drugs into my veins so that my body could gradually adjust to their toxicity, since she was too busy watching Lance's race. In one swift motion, she accidentally cranked up the chemo dispenser to "full force."

Although I was waving my hand like mad to get her attention, it was too late. Retching uncontrollably, vomit instantly poured out of me like a volcanic eruption. *That* got her attention fast. "Oops," she said sheepishly, the color rising in her checks. Clearly, my day had not gotten off to a very good start.

For me, one of the most crippling parts of having leukemia was continuous, physical pain, nothing like I had ever experienced, as if red hot, burning flames emanated from each nerve ending and places I didn't even know pain could exist—the bottom of my feet, my toes and ears, the back my neck, inside my brain—and that was on top of the ordinary places pain radiated from, including my head, chest, shoulders, and back.

Most days, my pain registered as a full "ten" on the hospital's "Zero-to-Ten Pain Scale," with zero being the lowest level and ten being the highest. Despite massive doses of narcotics, my insurmountable pain could not be controlled. I was told that the agonizing pain was a result of bone marrow cells breaking down from the leukemia treatments, but I didn't care about the cause. I simply needed to find a solution, and it was becoming more clear that a solution did not exist.

Profound bone pain is physically and mentally wearing. People have different pain tolerance levels, but for anyone, continual pain is unbearable. The rule of thumb at the cancer center was that a provider can't be afraid of giving a leukemia patient too much pain medication, despite the risk of addiction. My doctors were extremely reverent about this philosophy, and they encouraged me to stay as pain-free as possible. I was treated around the clock with a self-administering morphine pump, oxycodone, and many other pain medications. The side effects were that I slept a great deal, and *that,* at least, was a blessing.

For most leukemia patients, a surgically implanted, indwelling catheter stays implanted in the chest wall without complications for up to one year or longer. It is designed for this purpose, to spare the patient from continuous needle sticks and blood draws. Within several days of my catheter being inserted surgically, I developed tenderness, swelling, and redness around the site of my incision. It became clear that I had developed a fever, and because antibiotics had not swiftly eliminated the infection, that the catheter had to be surgically removed, and a new one reinserted.

Unfortunately, I had developed a painful, allergic reaction to the plastic catheter. An immediate, second operation, using a different manufacturer's material proved to be of no avail. Due to one unexplained infection after another at the site of the sutured area, I required five consecutive surgical operations over an eighteen-month period to continually replace infected lines. Four bold scars at my neck, and one at my groin, are proof to this day. If the disease itself does not lead to death, complications of this magnitude often do. My doctors had no choice other than to operate again and again. Five surgeries, one after another, began to take their toll on me, physically, mentally, and emotionally.

Another instance occurred some time toward the end of my second month of hospitalization, one night around two o'clock in the morning. A new burning infection developed again at the same tender site of my recently sutured, four-inch incision where my indwelling catheter was placed. The nursing shift had already thinned out since it was in the dead of night when patients are hopefully getting some sleep. This was the time the nurses tended to their mounds of paperwork, and generally hung out at the Nurses' Station down the hall.

The jagged pain startled me from my morphine-assisted sleep, and my body became hot with fever from a severe infection that was developing just below my neck. My breathing became more shallow each minute, as my throat and neck continued to swell. The base of my neck was swollen and raised to the extent that the six broad metal staples across my incision line began pulling out of my skin.

Not wanting to bother the night shift nurse, knowing she had her hands full already, I tried holding off pushing my red call button for another five minutes. Eventually, I did call the nurse. Twice. But it took her almost ten minutes to appear at my bedside. Taking one look, she agreed a doctor needed to come immediately to remove the sutures from the infected wound.

HEALING GRIEF

One hour went by, then two. The on-call doctor was unavailable to remove the stitches, as my pain, like a red hot iron, grew steadily worse. It turned out, there were too many other "life and death" cases that same night, and the hospital was short-staffed. Finally, after waiting more than two hours for what my nurse agreed was an emergency situation, an overly busy, distracted doctor sailed in. Curtly, she announced, "I hear from the nurse that you're annoyed I didn't come sooner. This place is so short-staffed tonight that it borders on dangerous." Needless to say, her remark was not comforting or professional.

With any warning at all, and far too busy to take a brief moment to calmly explain her plan, she lunged toward me like an enormous hawk going in for a kill. Aiming her surgical scissors right toward my swollen neck which was severely tender and hot to the touch, she jabbed the metal point into my skin to pry loose the deeply embedded, surgical steel staples, which she then yanked out of my neck. "The infection should be able to drain now," she muttered. Dropping the blood-stained scissors on her medical tray, she turned on her heels to leave.

"Wait!" I cried. "The job's not done. You just can't leave me like this. What about the pain? What about the infection?" Glaring at me with an inpatient look, I heard her mumble, "That's good enough for now," and she headed out into the hall. The skin on my throat was red, raw, and hot to the touch. I could not shake the pain no matter how hard I tried to distract myself. I suppose I should have been grateful that she at least opened my swollen airway so I could breathe.

Another harrowing incident, one which also seldom occurs, arose early on during my treatment. Lying in my hospital bed and strapped to the IV pole as always, this time I was getting a three-hour, vital infusion treatment of red blood cell platelets from a donor whose blood type, unfortunately, did not precisely match mine. Ten minutes into my cell infusion treatment, my teeth began to chatter as my body temperature plummeted. I could not stop shaking.

Awareness of my surroundings began to fade, and the groan of the transfusion machine began to grow dim. I wondered if I'd somehow fallen through ice. I could see that my hands and arms looked translucent, my nails and lips blue. Oxygen was being robbed from my cells at such a rapid pace that I could not get enough air into my lungs to breathe. My brain registered enough to say, "Reach over and hit that emergency red call button," but my fingertips would not comply. I could not move. The best way to explain this eerie sensation was that it felt like someone was pressing his hand against my nose and mouth to the point where I was ready to pass out. In fact, I was just about to do so. A moment later, the room grew dark.

Is this what was called an out-of-body experience? I was able to observe my body slowing down, but it seemed more like I was watching a scene on a movie screen. Maybe my fingers had reached that red button after all. Maybe that explained the sudden flurry of commotion, the team of white-clad team nurses frantically moving toward my face with an oxygen mask, yelling for me to focus on slowing down my breathing, demanding that I count with them, slowly, and then slower still. "Breathe in. One…Two…Now, breathe way out. One…Two…Three…Four."

After quickly assessing the severity of the situation, a second team of nurses appeared at my bedside with steaming hot blankets to instantly warm up my body temperature. I felt as if I was floating and fading away, and that I was as close to dying as I had ever experienced it. Something in me began rising toward the ceiling, I was sure of it. Was it my life force, or was it what people call their soul? I was relieved that the sensation was one of sheer tranquility—nothing hurt at all.

Once the oxygen began to work and I was breathing on my own, the doctor explained that I had experienced a rare, auto-immune reaction to my donor's platelets and collapsed into a medical condition called "rigors," one which requires emergency medical intervention.

That night, I wrote in my journal:

They call it rigors. I couldn't breathe. I felt like I was dying. There's wasn't enough air in my lungs, and my brain was turning to mush. I couldn't think, the room was spinning, then the images weren't recognizable at all. I heard the nurses' voices ever so faintly, although they were in my face, in my ears, talking to me loudly and clearly. "YOU ARE IN RIGORS…TRY TO FOCUS ON OUR WORDS. TRY TO LISTEN. TRY TO LOOK AT US AND HEAR OUR VOICES. YOU NEED TO BRING YOUR HEART RATE DOWN. LET'S COUNT TOGETHER, YOU CAN DO THIS. ONE…TWO…THREE…FOUR…" I thought, Oh-my-God, what's happening to me?

As a result of my treatments, I had little immune system left, which put me at tremendous risk of infection from others. Patients with a low white blood cell count, a consequence from chemotherapy, must be extremely cautious about impending infection. There was great concern that environmental germs could lead to grave consequences. Because of this very real health concern, physical contact in the hospital without mask or gloves was discouraged.

Hand holding, hugging, kissing, the basic acts of everyday intimacy became a special privilege, and only after great precautions were taken. The side of the bed I had shared with Ken for two decades lay empty. Doctors, nurses, social workers, even my family, were required to wash their hands vigorously with soap and water before they were allowed to enter my room. The need for intimacy hung in balance with the real medical concern that I might get another infection if people came too close.

By the end of the fourth week, I developed painful, oozing mouth sores on the entire floor of my mouth, as well as the roof of my mouth, even ones that extended down my throat, as a result of one of the chemotherapy drugs I was taking and needed to continue if I was planning to stay alive. The raw sores tasted and smelled foul, like metal and blood in my mouth. Was this some kind of cruel endurance test, and the exact reason why Ken promised from the start that he'd take the journey with me so I wouldn't feel scared and alone?

In the beginning, let's say during the first two cycles of grueling treatments while living in the hospital, I did a pretty good job maintaining my conviction that I could get through all my cycles of treatments with a brave face using every ounce of courage I could muster. After lying awake for hours in the middle of the night in my room, feeling lonely, and praying the doctors could give me stronger pain medication, I began to sob. I knew I had yet another severe infection that was out of control, and I couldn't handle one more problem. I had reached my limit.

The eventual conclusion was that I had developed an allergic reaction to the chemotherapy, but there was truly nothing that could be done about the problem. This kept me wondering, would this happen again tomorrow? The pain meds weren't effective, and my mouth was swollen with infection. As a last resort, the doctors, hoping to try something different, treated me with high doses of steroids. After twenty-four hours, the swelling resolved and the pain diminished.

As soon as the steroids were stopped, however, a mysterious new pain and swelling developed in my right leg, beginning at the base and working its way all the way up to my hip. After succumbing to yet another MRI scan to help detect any bleeding that might be the cause of my pain, for the first time, I felt panicked in that closed chamber. A doctor from the rheumatology department was also called in to figure out the cause of this inflammatory process. My disorder was diagnosed as fasciitis, an infection or inflammation of the fibrous tissues which surround the muscles. Now I had both a disease and a disorder. Things were going from bad to worse.

A report from my medical chart reads as follows:

"The patient, a forty-two year old female, received induction therapy with daunorubicin, VP-16 and ARA-C. Her hospital stay was complicated by line infection, allo immunization to platelets, tid platelet transfusions and a right interior leg compartment syndrome, DIC, and tumor lysis. At the completion of her induction chemotherapy, she then underwent three cycles of high dose ARA-C consolidation

complicated by conjunctivitis."

The leg pain was so intense, it felt as if my bones were breaking. Unable to contain the physical pain, I was screaming and begging the nurses and doctors to do something, *anything* to please make it stop. Ken, watching me in such distress, became frantic and did all he could to try to get me help quickly. The highest level of morphine would not relieve the pain, and thus, high-dose steroids were restarted. The continual use of steroids I was given was dangerously high, but truly, there was no alternative. No one had forewarned me about these sorts of terrifying complications when I signed on the dotted line to undergo treatments. There was no choice if I wanted to live.

Losing Hope

THE OVERBEARING PHYSICAL pain sapped me of my mental and emotional energy to stay focused on the task, and gradually, I ran out of endurance. Additionally, the overbearing psychological distress resulting from the series of medical misfortunes and mishaps continued to occur, about which I felt basically silenced or not permitted to talk about freely. I felt I had no choice but to grin and bear it. The accumulation of these frequent, debilitating experiences tested my resolve beyond which I was capable. These horrible experiences were the ones that made me finally buckle under the pressure.

With each passing week, I became more and more despondent, and I begged my doctor to stop my cancer treatments. My spirit was worn down, and I couldn't handle another day. The strong mental toughness I had developed and sustained during my first few months of cancer treatments was weakening. The physical and emotional perseverance required to overcome these atypical medical emergencies, in addition to the "ordinary" difficult cancer treatments themselves, was no longer there.

All I kept thinking to myself is that this was just the *first* five-week inpatient stay. No way could I possibly do this for *three more* five-week inpatient cycles. My doctors explained that if I simply gave up after this first cycle was over, with certainty I would die. If I didn't go through with the next three cycles, the hard work I had endured during the first cycle would have been a waste of time.

Although knowledge can be a helpful tool, in my case, from the very beginning, I knew too much about all the devastating things that could go wrong. Being the spouse of a cancer doctor, I was aware all along of my slim chances of survival.

I was ashamed of not being strong enough to go that final mile—the last five-week inpatient round—even though I knew I would be persevering in the name of our children, our parents, and my husband. Grief continued to snowball. There was no one with whom I felt safe to share except Ken and perhaps a close friend, but I could see that they were getting worn down, too, from all of my complaints. I became more depressed with each passing day. Walking into my hospital room would mean confronting a defeated, upset, and angry patient. As a result, some people, even my own family members and friends, as well as nurses, doctors, residents and interns would often stay back a few yards with trepidation and concern. Some knew better than to proceed, expecting grief on the other side of the door.

I was hurt when the doctors backed away from my hospital room, and I knew it was because I could no longer be Little Miss Sunshine, upbeat, optimistic, and pleasant to be around. I was no longer their "good patient," grateful for their medical care. No longer their success case and source of pride, I noticed how they hung back at my doorway instead of coming into my room and sitting with me for a moment or two. Did they think my depression was contagious?

Imagine how disgusting I felt, and how sad their withdrawal made me feel. Five feet six inches, and down to one hundred pounds. Sallow complexion, the whites of my eyes turned faint yellow, stray wisps of a dozen or so hairs on my head that I was told not to shave or else I'd risk infection. I felt many must be repulsed, and I could not blame them. Feeling isolated from the most important people in life was one of the hardest things to bear. What I craved was just the opposite—a warm, caring hand on my arm or shoulder, that precious human touch at a time when I needed it most, a gentle word or two—so that despite my gruesome appearance and feeling so hideous inside, I was still respected and valued.

Giving up was an embarrassment. I loathed feeling like a coward and a failure, especially to those who harshly reminded me to think of my children first. "What will they do without you? If not for yourself, you must carry on for them." Guilt! Nor was I the person who had always been there for them, the steady one they could always count on for compassion and support. Gone was that noble feeling I used to carry like a torch when others looked up to me as a source of personal hope and inspiration. I felt like a crestfallen military hero whose medals had been ripped off her chest.

My resentment had built up against Ken to an unhealthy level after feeling forced against my will to comply with the daily outpatient treatments required to keep my cancer at bay between inpatient sessions. "It's time for your daily Procrit injection to boost your red blood cell count," he would insist. On the one hand, he was kind enough to offer to give them to me in the comfort of our home. Yet I hated getting those painful injections in my stomach every day for five months. However, a worse alternative was sitting in a medical oncologist's waiting room nearly every day for five months to have my injections done by a busy lab technician.

Family and friends urged me to hang on, promising me that I'd feel better soon, once my anti-depressant kicked in. My doctor reassured me over and over again that my depression was not my fault, as I shamefully convinced myself it was. I couldn't stop beating myself up. If I had just been mentally stronger through my cancer treatments, then I wouldn't have fallen apart emotionally. To this, my doctor replied, "No, Joan, you're mistaken. We know that depression is caused by biochemical changes in the brain. Your cancer treatments were the chief culprit for causing the chemical imbalance in your brain. Your depression is not a matter of you not being strong enough, nor is your depression your fault," the doctor said.

Despite everyone's efforts to make me feel better, depression took hold like a dark fog. It was as if an ominous, gray cloud had set in, growing bigger each day, billowing with gray smoke. I definitely flunked cancer. I thought that I must be the only cancer patient in the world who ended up clinically depressed and couldn't "make it" emotionally.

◄ **HEALING GRIEF**

Defining depression can be hard. The body and mind are integrated and work together; each one impacts the other. What happens to all those toxic emotions—worry, fear, anger, regret, sadness—which a dying patient feels, but is not permitted to disclose? These feelings must go somewhere. They just don't fly away into the atmosphere and disappear. Sometimes, they build up inside and gather so much force that they begin to take on a life of their own. Because I did not feel safe or supported to express my painful feelings, they turned inward.

If my depression could have talked, it would have said, "No one listens to my opinion anymore; my voice is useless. You can't tell me what to do anymore because I've shut down. I have carved a far-away place for myself where no one can disagree with me or force me to do things against my will. I have turned my whole self inward and have disappeared. Finally, I found a perfect place to hide. You can try to argue, but it won't make a difference, because I am no longer here. I have gone to a place where no one can find me, hidden away in my own cocoon, my entire being shut down."

Life was so painful that dying seemed like the only way out, an act of mercy. Worse than any punishment I had known, there was an unbearable powerlessness. There was no way out.

An entry from my journal reads:

What's wrong with me? I am a disappointment to everyone in my life, and I have no one to blame but myself. I cannot talk about what a coward I am, because I feel so ashamed. I am no longer that former, put-together self. That person has disappeared. She is completely lost. Gone.

No one wants to hear that I feel like giving up. They won't tolerate it. "You shouldn't feel so hopeless and that you can't go on. Don't talk like that. We need you. You can't give up." My voice, on the other hand, is utterly silenced.

I want to try to explain in words what depression feels like so you can understand. Depression is a whole body pain, physical and

LOSING HOPE

mental. The pain is unexplainable unless you have ever been through it, which I hope you never, ever will. Unlike the worst migraine you've ever had where the pain is localized to just one part of your body, your head alone, depression permeates your whole body, pulsating in every single cell from head to toe.

As opposed to a headache where only part of the head is throbbing, the physical pain of depression grips the entire brain as if it's being held in a vise. Imagine removing your brain and holding it in your hands. Now, squeeze it with all your might. It is so swollen that it's about to explode. Or imagine a heavy jackhammer pounding on the delicate, soft tissue of your brain. The pain won't stop.

What I've been able to explain is just a fraction of the pain that invades the body when depression sets in. Depression feels as if a thermostat in the brain has gone haywire. Have you ever had the chicken pox or measles with a fever of 104 degrees, and your body was wet and clammy, feeling hot one minute, and cold the next? You don't feel like yourself anymore. Your face is white as a ghost; you have dark brown circles under your eyes. Nerves inside the body go haywire too. It feels like there are thousands of tiny spiders crawling madly on every nerve ending.

The mental pain of depression exacerbates the physical pain. The aching, pounding, intensely-hot then freezing-cold, crawling-spider-sensation is only half the problem. My mind plays a broken record that wears on my nerves and just won't stop. I've heard people try to describe the annoying sensation of tinnitus, or ringing in one's ear. Some say it's so aggravating that it keeps them awake at night. My depressed thoughts keep hammering away like mad. "My life is not worth living. I'm hurting everyone I love. They would be better off without me. I'll never get better." Although I try, I can't turn down the maddening noise. I try to think distracting thoughts, but depressive thoughts keep taking over. "Maybe I'll be surprised and start feeling better soon — No, I'll never get better."

Imagine being forced to walk barefoot on smoldering hot coals, while searing pain shoots through the souls of your feet, flames *melting away each layer of skin, each nerve ending exploding in pain. Screams of pain echo in my brain. I realize with horror, they are my own. Every one of my cells burns like a raging fire. This sensation of depression feels like being burned alive, like hell on earth, with no way to put out the fire. Stop this pain. Anything would be better than this. Death would be a relief.*

Dear God, if you really are there, as some people say you are, and if you are truly good, not evil, why you would let me suffer this way? Isn't it enough that I had to suffer through my cancer treatments, and now, this depression, too? My mind explodes from the violent, shooting flames. My body is engulfed by fiery red and orange explosions, and helpless screams echo in my ears. Feeling as if I'd been doused with gasoline and set on fire, I beg someone to relieve me of pain. Someone, help me. Listen, I beg you. Why aren't you listening? Is there no one to help?

I call out, but no one answers my cries. Why don't they come to my side? They turn away, for they cannot bear watching me in such uncontrollable pain. No one listens to my merciful pleading to put out the fire. The raging fire consumes my very soul. I've been pushed beyond the brink of sanity. I beg and plead. Dear God, why are you letting me suffer in this hell on earth? Is this part of your design, you cruel, unforgiving monster? There is no way out, and no one comes. There's no escape. Like a fetus, I curl up inside myself, the only place I can find to hide.

I just couldn't bear the anguish anymore; it was humanly impossible. My cries went unanswered, and the fire kept burning. There was no escape except for sleep, an all-too-brief respite that flew by in what unfortunately felt like a fleeting moment in time. Reading, watching TV, listening to music, and meditating all took up too much energy, and I couldn't keep lying there suffering this way. As soon as Ken would leave the room, I couldn't get the medicine bottle of Klonopin, a fast-acting anti-anxiety medication, open quickly enough. I knew I was going against my doctor's orders to take more than the prescribed amount, but anyone experiencing these symptoms would do what I did. How easy for them to say, "I'm sorry, but you can't take your medicine more often than every twelve hours." The moment I woke up, I'd think to myself, "Oh My God, how can I possibly be awake again so soon. I only had a brief moment of relief, and now I'm not allowed to take another pill for twelve more hours."

The only way out was in. Though I knew I should not, I would reach for another pill. Within seconds, the all-consuming fire would immediately die down. My breathing would quiet, and it felt as though a gentle breeze had settled around me. Sleep, come quickly. Wrap yourself around me, so all will be quiet and still. Finally. Relief.

I escaped to my bed. Night and day, it was my place of refuge, the only solution for calming my racing, destructive thoughts. I stayed upstairs to be as far as possible from the lively pace of the family down below. There in my upstairs bedroom, in one far end of the house, I managed to close myself off from the outside world. I pulled my blanket up tight, being sure to cover my face to block out any daylight peeking in. I lay in the darkness where all was silent and serene, like a bear cub hibernating through the long, frozen winter.

Many times throughout the day, Ken and others tried to coax me to come out of hiding. I begged them, "Please, just let the pain stop. Just let me close my eyes and drift off to sleep." My bedroom was the steady place I escaped to. I kept the shades drawn, and in the serenity of my dark room, life was quiet, silent, and still. Under the protection of my warm, embracing blanket, I leaned my heavy head against my downy, soft pillow, my shoulders and back pressed into the warmth of the mattress, a baby chick nestled in the fluff of its mother's under belly.

I arranged my aching body perfectly, until I was nestled comfortably and securely, longing for the pressure in my brain to disappear. Like a newborn baby, swaddled in a soft, warm baby blanket, the silk on the hem felt smooth against my skin. My shades were drawn, my eyes were closed, and I became enveloped by the tranquility.

My mother called my house and demanded I speak with her. First

HEALING GRIEF

crying, then wailing with the jagged pain only a mother can experience when she loses a child, it is her shrieks that jarred me into some sensibility. "Joan, I need you!" she cried in a voice that came from a deep place in her belly. "You *must* get out of that bed. I am lost without you. I need you in my life."

It was her words that hit me. They touched me so deeply. Her cries were that of the raw pain she felt in having lost her daughter to depression and despair. Until then, I did not believe that my depression, a symbolic death in a way, mattered much to anyone anymore. It was her heart-wrenching, guttural plea that jarred me from my makeshift grave. Her desperation for my love awakened a bit of flame that must have still been hiding within me.

The Thanksgiving holiday was coming up that weekend, and despite my mother's desperate appeals, I simply could not go. I had become more and more depressed each week, and I wished the rest of my family would just celebrate without me. Couldn't they let me find peace? I wished they would let me take my anti-anxiety medication, put my throbbing head on my soft pillow, close my eyes and drift away from this reality.

I grew accustomed to Ken's threats, "I can't stand this one more minute. You can't keep doing this to me," as though he was the one lying in bed, the one in such anguish. The tone in his voice was different this time. Forcefully, he yelled, "Get out of that bed! It is unfair to our children and to me that you keep lying there!" Even in my deep despair, I knew Ken was right.

I had hit rock bottom. I couldn't go lower than this. When did my depression first take hold—was it during my first inpatient stay or was it during my second? Maybe it was the third? I lost track. The days and the treatments seemed to blend into one. The sequence of events melded into one l-o-n-g nightmare.

I retreated to my bed, lying in the dark with the covers pulled tightly over my head. I lay as quiet and still as a sleeping butterfly, cradled by the warmth and softness of my sheets. My bed had transformed into a soothing, enveloping hideaway, a cocoon that allowed

LOSING HOPE

me to shield myself from the outside world, and run away from future treatments or demands to keep on going no matter what. Lying in bed, I found a way to disconnect myself from the overwhelming demands in my life. Sinking under the covers, my negative energy contained, I lay relatively undisturbed. Hiding under these billowy sheets was the only strategy I could think of to relieve myself of my aching depression.

After several weeks with no improvement, I was told by my family and my doctor that my depression was not getting any better, and they were admitting me to a psychiatric hospital. Lying in bed at home was no longer an option. I was being forced against my will. "You have no choice," my husband said. It was like heading into a torture chamber. The same powerlessness and isolation I felt reminded me of when I was hospitalized for my dismal leukemia treatments.

I wrote in my journal at the psychiatric hospital:

I am still so depressed that my husband has admitted me to an inpatient psychiatric ward, so that the doctors can adjust my depression and anxiety medications to give me relief. They say I have a mental illness, and now, I must be locked up like a criminal. It is also essential that I be weaned off my pain medication that I have become addicted to, because it is the only thing I can do to dull the psychic pain of depression. I absolutely do not want to be here. Haven't I suffered enough with cancer treatments and depression? These doctors think they can lock me behind bars, just because they are so powerful and almighty.

I yell and cry and beg to be let out, but all sneer and look away. There is not one soul who cares about me here, and I'm fighting for my life. I am trapped in hell. Or maybe this is the Purgatory I was terrified to learn about in early childhood. I must be destined to be persecuted by the Authorities, banished from all of society, held captive in some remote, barren structure of gray cement, just as I imagine frightful lepers and mentally ill people were once locked away in sanitariums. Defective, discarded human beings, and now I'm one, too. I can actually feel the sorrowful aching of an empty, broken heart, and the anguish from feeling so desperately alone.

With each degrading experience and act of physician coerciveness on this inpatient mental unit, I am feeling less human each day. My opportunities to make decisions for myself, including when I am allowed to eat, use the bathroom, or have privacy in my room have all been taken away. I am at the mercy of this powerful psychiatric institution.

Once I stepped into this place, I became a number, not an individual. I am treated the same as every other patient, all labeled mentally ill. Powerless, feeble minded, irresponsible, and mentally disturbed. How I ended up here in the first place seems inconsequential to the staff. It doesn't seem to matter who I am, or what my life story is that led me to this place. Locked up, trapped here, I feel punished, a menace to society. Are psychiatric institutions more like prisons, or are they places designed for one to get well? One thing's clear: psychiatric professionals have absolute authority to diagnose and treat individuals against their will and to enforce obedience.

Like a child, I search for my mother everywhere, calling out her name. "Mom, come get me!" Fear grips me because I can't find her anywhere. I look for someone else with compassion, anyone willing to reach out to me with tenderness, and above all, hope. But no one comes. There are no arms to hold me, no strong chest on which to lay my head. My family must hate me; why else would they force me to leave home and suffer this way? No one can possibly fathom or understand the despair of solitude and fright that has become my torturous lot in life. There is no one who can relieve my excruciating mental suffering.

Similar to my experience in the inpatient cancer unit, my stay at the psychiatric unit was painfully lonely. Once again, I felt as if I had no control in important decision-making that affected my well-being. When I expressed resentment at being forced to go there against my will, my feelings were dismissed. This was precisely how I felt when

I was forced against my will to be admitted for a fourth cycle of cancer treatments. In each case, I said the very same words: "Enough is enough!" But no one seemed to listen.

I had lost my resolve to bear any further treatments, because even the greatest dose of morphine wasn't enough to dim the crippling, bone-wrenching pain. My surrender felt shameful and indicated a loss of self-respect, a sign of weakness of character, failing all those in my life. Unable to express myself without being ridiculed or misunderstood, feeling disdained by hospital staff during my cancer treatments, my self-esteem plummeted. Being locked away like a prison inmate, not permitted to take part in my children's events, help them with their school work, or drive them to their dance classes, I felt like I had been sent away from the life I loved.

Being readmitted for a fourth cycle of cancer treatments was beyond my personal limits, and then, several months later, family members insisted I become hospitalized for mental illness. The same anger surged in me again, this time with a greater intensity than before, because the two assaults to my ego merged into one. In both cases, first as a patient in the cancer unit, and then, as a patient in the psychiatric ward, I was forced to go. "You have no choice," I was told. In the case of my psychiatric hospitalization, only select family members were permitted to visit. I believed my family and friends had developed mistrust in my ability to bounce back. I certainly had.

Letters to My Grief Companion

FINALLY, ONE OF Ken's many efforts to help pull me out of this deep depression made a difference. After my stay in the psychiatric hospital, which didn't do much good, he tried introducing me to countless therapists so that I could find a someone with whom I could connect. After weeks of desperation and even a brief consideration of electroshock therapy, I finally met my professional grief companion, a psychotherapist practicing in a private office. She became my primary connection to the world.

My journal entries gradually became letters to her:

It feels like you are my main connection to the world outside this fortress, the person who persists in helping me fight for my rights to get out of this place. Locked behind bars, I feel like I am nothing but an empty shell. You still believe in me, pledge your alliance, show me how much you care, and urge me to hang on. You promise you'll stick with me until my depression lifts, no matter what. You are my one source of hope.

At the psychiatric hospital, there is one phone at the end of the hall, and the nurses seem to watch with amusement as we all run frantically toward it every time it rings. It's a race they've never needed to run. As we end our brief phone call each day, you ask if it's all right to call me the next day, and the day after that one, and the day after that. I am taken aback by your simple request, touched by your thoughtfulness to wonder about my needs, my desires. Imagine that! In this frightening place where I'm held against my will, you are the only person making a concerted effort to keep my dignity intact. I wish you had the power to get me out of this place altogether.

I am so hopeless and depressed, most days I cannot bring myself to talk when you call, and I tell you so. Some days I just don't have the energy to pick up at all. My silence and hopelessness don't stop you from calling nevertheless. When I hear your voice, and when you call me by my first name, something no one does in this place, you make me feel as if I still matter. You treat me as a human being with dignity, tenderness, and compassion, the only one left in my life who does so.

I am terrified, and I despise my family and doctors for forcing me to come here. I cry and scream, "Let me go home. I need to get out." I can't bear being confined another minute. Can't they see that forcing me to stay here, away from my children and family and friends, is making me slip farther and farther away from reality? I have lost hope in myself, save for the fact that you are determined to somehow keep my spirit alive.

I am a solitary dingy, adrift in a vast, dark sea, fighting hard to cling to life. With no land in sight, I worry I might never be rescued from these murky waters of misery and suffering. Knowing how detached I feel from the rest of humanity, you continue to show your care and commitment to help me get well. You are a constant anchor in my life, the one person left I can lean on for strength and hope.

You are kind enough to take an hour off from seeing your other therapy patients back at your office, and instead, you come to see me in the mental ward, to be with me for a short while. But, now our time is up, and you must go. How can you leave me here, when you know I am so frightened and alone? Why don't you tell people I'm not crazy, and that I don't belong here? You explain there are no adequate inpatient mental health facilities nearby for people like me, and that you feel badly for forcing me to stay.

So now, even you abandon me, leaving me holed up in this hellish place. I feel small and scared, like a caged rat, forever in a frenzy to

⊰ **HEALING GRIEF**

find its way out. I am frightened for my safety, unprotected from the other inmates who scare me. I can't breathe in this place. There is no fresh air. It's as if I am being buried alive! Let me out!

Ever so slowly you say, "Goodbye, Joan." I am stunned. Then, you turn your back to me and start walking down that long, dark corridor toward the exit door. As you reach your destination, you hesitate for just a moment. Then you turn to face me, and your eyes lock with mine. Suddenly, you look the other way. As you punch in the security code, I know what comes next. It's that dreadful sound, the thud of the heavy, locked door. Lucky you! You are free to head out into the sunshine, into the hustle and bustle of life outside these locked doors, whereas, I am trapped.

Is my mind playing tricks on me? I vividly recall the elevator door closing with the same heavy thud as I rode up to the fifth-floor oncology inpatient unit, that very first day of my inpatient cancer treatments. The same dreadful feeling rises up in me now as it did back then. I'm trapped. I feel doomed. Please don't leave me here. But the heavy locked door shuts tight, and you are gone.

I want to tell you what it feels like being sane in an insane place. I am confined like a prisoner. Two steel doors, one after the other, locked and monitored around the clock to prevent escape. Metal bars hang on the windows as a reminder that there's no way out. No way to escape. The windows panes are darkened to obscure the view, making it impossible to know if the world is still out there, and whether life still exists as we know it, outside these walls.

Now that I am locked behind these barred windows and bolted doors, sleeping on a flimsy rubber cot, I realize how good I had it back at home. It's impossible to put a price on freedom. Mine has been taken away, and I'd give anything to get it back. My heart aches to be discharged from this dungeon. If someone doesn't let me out, I'll go mad. Someone! Anyone! Can't you hear me? You've got to get me out…I am dying in here. I can't stay one more day. Simple freedom is all I crave—fresh air, sunshine on my face, wind blowing through my hair. At least I have my journal, I remind myself.

LETTERS TO MY GRIEF COMPANION

At mealtimes, we are instructed to pick up a white styrofoam tray and plastic utensils, both of which I despise. We mental misfits march single file, clutching our flimsy trays to our chest. On any given day, there might be ten of us, standing in line, one behind the other, waiting for our turn. We practice this daily ritual three times a day, breakfast, lunch, and dinner. No snacks between meals. The heavy, uneven dollop of grayish mashed potatoes sinks into the upper left partition, bending the whole right side of my tray. This balancing feat is so comical that I begin to wonder whether there's a group of amused photographers laughing at us behind their hidden camera lenses. What a pitiful sight.

The ten of us finally collect our food and sit down together, as required, in the cafeteria. This camaraderie over a shared experience is as normal as life gets in this place. Despite our vast differences and degrees of mental illness or wellness, there is a small comfort in the experiences we have in common. It is the mouth opening, food-chewing-and-swallowing, filling-the-empty-belly experience we collectively share. I try not to listen as my housemates compare notes about the worst homeless shelters in town, or the number of their past suicide attempts and hospital admissions.

Something is terribly wrong with this picture. I may be deeply depressed and anxious, but I am not certified crazy. How do I know? The one major difference between me and the others in this cheap hotel is that everyone else feels protected and safe. They proclaim how glad they are to be here. "They give us three square meals a day, and a clean bed and hot shower. I don't get any of that out on the street."

Of the twelve of us that are hospitalized this particular week, many are homeless, and most are former psychiatric patients thrown into the streets after money dried up for federally subsidized mental institutions. I live under the same roof with a patient I call the Coconut Man. He does not stand or walk; he crawls on all fours. Like an animal prowling around for food, he crawls on his hands and knees across the floor in the common dining area, all the while smacking his forehead against the unforgiving concrete floor. He cannot stop himself.

The Coconut Man is psychotic to the point that he does not speak or acknowledge our presence. As if on some kind of mission, he crawls and smacks, crawls and smacks, crawls and smacks. Picture for a moment a coconut with its dark outer shell. Now take hold of this coconut, then smack it over and over again against the ground, until finally, liquid trickles out from the thin crevices of the cracked shell. The skin on the Coconut Man's swollen, misshapen forehead is worn away, exposing filmy pink tissue and oozing pus. I feel a mixture of empathy, disgust, and complete terror as he heads towards me.

Sitting at the dining room table at mealtime, he comes alive, turning into a greedy cannibal before our eyes. His lips part hungrily, exposing infected gums and decayed, broken teeth. In a starving frenzy, he suddenly thrusts himself across the table to where I am sitting. His open mouth lowers towards my plate, revealing his matted hair, covered in lice. Next, his gnarly fingers grab the food from my plate. Stuffing it wildly into his mouth, he grunts and snorts. Just an inch away from him, I'm afraid he'll bite me, too.

Is this what will become of me one day? If he has been placed here, and I have been placed here, does that mean I am crazy, too? If I am forced to stay here much longer, I'm sure I will lose my mind. A psychiatric inpatient ward in an inner-city hospital is no place for a patient who is not insane. And it's certainly not a healing place for a woman who's confronted more than enough trauma from her experiences as a patient on an inpatient cancer ward.

Nobody agrees to discharge me from the place, so I stay locked up against my will. I have no choice. Like an angry tiger in a zoo, I pace anxiously back and forth. The more I beg the staff to be released, the more the observant doctors remark how agitated I've become. "Mrs. Miller is having difficulty managing her anger today. She will have to discuss her feelings in 'group.'"

Can't you see I don't belong here? I don't fit in. I'm not one of them. We are worlds apart. Like a globe tipped on an axis, being confined in an inpatient mental ward shifts my center twenty degrees out-of-sync with the rest of the world. Forced to stay here, locked away with all the others, I'm afraid I'll become crazy, just like them.

All others have bailed ship but you. You promise to stick with me no matter. You are my lifeline, my promise of hope for the future. Time and again, you've proven that you'll hang on for as long as it takes for me to get well. You promise not to give up, the thing I dread most. Although my faith that life will improve has disappeared, I still cling to your hope and reassurance that depression lifts, if I will just hang on.

The next day, I write:

I've managed to make it through another sleepless night behind bars. My psychiatrist says he won't allow me to leave this place until my anxiety and depression medications have been properly adjusted. I am overdue for my medication, and my anxiety peaked hours ago. Now I pace back and forth like the Coconut Man. I'm experiencing a withdrawal from Klonopin, a medication that my doctor says he is no longer willing to prescribe because I've become addicted. At the precise moment each four-hour dose wears off, the murderous sensation of akathisia—spiders crawling up and down my spine—returns.

My doctor discovers me at the nurses' station, hands clasped in prayer. Like an overwrought drug addict, I plead for one last hit. How humiliating to have stooped this low. "No more Klonopin," he insists. "Although it makes you feel better instantly, we must switch you to a different medicine that is not addictive. Terror washes through me as the thought of quitting "cold turkey" resonates through my brain. How did I manage to end up here, and how will I survive?

It's mandatory group therapy time again. There are fourteen of us in all today, cramped in a small room with no windows, with stark white walls and stark white floors. The lone fluorescent light flickers overhead as the intermittent neon blues and yellows dance on the stark white ceiling. No one is in a hurry to talk today. Some fidget in their chairs, trying to settle into a comfortable seating position. Others lean back and close their eyes, blocking out the reality of the grim

HEALING GRIEF

situation we have found ourselves in. Finally, we settle down, ready to begin. The room is perfectly silent. We watch and listen.

"Who would like to start today?" our group leader asks. No one raises their hand. "Perhaps Teresa would be willing to share a little more about growing up in her house with her father?" Teresa sits on the opposite side of the circle facing me. Only six feet away, she is visibly shaken, as if a lightning bolt had shot right through her. She becomes clearly agitated, frantically shaking her head back and forth. Then she is chided by another group member sitting across the room. "C'mon, Teresa, it'll make you feel better to talk about your father and how the son of a bitch used to rape and torture you." No way, Teresa lets us know, her eyes shut tight.

Our group leader steers the conversation away and becomes engaged with a different client. My eyes, however, are still on Teresa. I watch as she gazes down, transfixed, while turning over her forearm, exposing its underside—taut, translucent, like the throbbing underbelly of a freshly caught flounder. Next, she transforms the sharp metal tip in the clasp of her watchband into an instrument of war. Mechanically, the fingers on her right hand unbuckle the clasp of the watchstrap on her left. She releases the buckle at the end of the strap, exposing the sharp metal prong in the middle.

Carefully positioning the clasp, she gauges the tip deeply into her flesh, until tiny bubbles of dark red blood rises to the surface. Starting at the wrist, moving upward, Teresa bears down, slicing the metal blade through the firm skin until tiny rivulets of fresh blood bubble up into nice, neat parallel lines, each row four inches long, like a farmer irrigating his crop.

She focuses only on the cutting, slicing the skin, again and again. Self-mutilation seems to calm her otherwise agitated state of being. The searing physical pain must anesthetize her raw emotional pain. Like a Buddha in still meditation, her breathing finally settles into a pattern. I watch her chest expand and contract, her breath flowing steadily in and out.

The contents of my stomach start to rise, as I am forced to watch her commit this violent act, the words spill out of me. "I think I'm going to be sick." I don't want to stay here. Haven't I been through enough trauma from all my cancer treatments? Doesn't anyone realize I came into this place without my usual resolve and personal strength to begin with, and now I must witness this!

"I have to leave." I need to go back to my room so I don't have to watch this for one more minute. "That would be a rude thing to do, Joan," the group leader insists. "You're being disrespectful." I lower my head and close my eyes. There's no place else to hide.

Being sane in an insane place only adds to my desperation and panic about being forced to stay. I am an inpatient on this psychiatric ward, therefore, my individual rights of freedom have been taken away. I must do what I am told. I am locked up with Teresa as a roommate, with no means of escape. Her pain, blood, and torment wash through me, and all that is left to do is close my eyes and pray. Please, someone hear my cries. I am becoming crazy in here. Someone let me out.

The next day, I write:

It is mandatory group therapy time again, and today, group members decide to share stories about their suicide attempts. We are seated in a tight circle, shoulder to shoulder. The group leader explains that we happen to be an unusually large group in a small space. She motions for us to pull up several worn chairs perched in the back corners of the room so there's enough room for everyone in this cramped circle. Patients must follow all rules. No questions asked. If patients are uncooperative, there are negative consequences such as a suspension of a daily fifteen-minute break in a fenced-in area outside the hospital.

I have to find a way out, or at the very least, figure out a way to earn the privilege of a fresh air break. As each day goes by where I am forced to stay locked up, this lingering stale air and these cement walls close in on me farther. When I tell the group leader in an angry

HEALING GRIEF

voice that I feel like I can't breathe in this place, he tells me to calm down and to stop getting worked up.

But wait. I couldn't help notice that sometime yesterday morning and again in the afternoon, several patients left the room for a little while. Accompanied by a supervisor, they filed out the door. I watched them reach toward their breast or pants pockets, fumbling for their cigarettes. That's it! I'll become a cigarette smoker. Although I gave up the filthy habit twenty years ago, I need to take up smoking again, right this very minute. Then I, too, will be able to take legitimate outdoor breaks with the others. Quickly, I stand up and approach one of my fellow inmates. "Mind if I borrow a smoke," I wink. "Sure thing, help yourself," he says, as he places a cigarette in my hand.

A few minutes later, I've escaped. We smokers huddle together in a small outdoor courtyard outside the confines of the hospital walls. Smoke billows through my nostrils and into my lungs, and though I'm not getting the fresh air break I imagined, I'll gladly settle for the cool autumn wind blowing through my hair and the warmth of the sun shining on my face. Heaven.

If the doctors won't let me get out of here, the least they could do is let me sit by myself in my room with the company of a book. Being forced to attend group meetings hour after hour and confined to a dark, dreary room with no windows, is degrading. "You don't have to contribute, but you must attend," the group leader announces. Oh joy, so you're saying that I'm allowed to sit here quietly as long as I do so in a respectful fashion?

I feel like I'm back in kindergarten, being forced to follow rules designed to socialize children to become responsible human beings. "Sit quietly. Stop fidgeting in your seat. Pay attention." This authoritative model works successfully with youngsters because of the inherent power difference between children and adults. Children expect to be disciplined. They naturally learn if they are cooperative and obey the teacher's rules, they will be praised and rewarded for good behavior. Alternatively, they learn by experience that they will be punished if they do not comply with their teacher's demands.

Being forced to listen repeatedly to desperate stories from strangers who've come to their wit's end feels too close to home. Will I be pushed over the edge, too? Am I next in line? The door between sane and insane swings precariously. Even sane individuals, at times, can begin to fear they might be crossing the line between mental health and mental illness. I feel like I might lose my mind if I keep having to sit here and listen.

Why don't my doctors listen when I beg them to leave? I insist that I have to get out of this place and go home. How soon will they let me go? And what will happen to me when I get there? How can I gain the trust of my family again? Who else in the world will take care of my kids and love them as much as I do? When will I ever feel good again? Will I ever get my life back to normal and how? Will my marriage survive? What will become of me? Will I be able to save face with my family and friends and community after losing their respect, or will I end up being a homeless bag lady sitting out on a street corner? How will I survive and move forward with my life?

Another journal entry reads:

As I look out the tiny window of my hospital room down onto the street below, I can see that life continues as usual for everyone else on this sunny afternoon outside these hospital walls. Inside this hospital, however, I've convinced myself I may be in trouble in a whole different way. In the past few days, the same sharp familiar pains I experienced when I was first diagnosed with leukemia have come creeping back into my spine. With each successive day, the pain has become more intense, first in my lower back, then upper back, then my shoulders and neck; pains so fierce, there is nothing I can think to do to get relief. Each day as my pain gets worse, it becomes harder to stay on top of it. Tylenol, meditation, visualization, lying down, standing up, walking, standing still—nothing works. I simply cannot get comfortable.

I have also been aware of, but have been trying to push back into the recess of my mind, one or two dark bruises that I found on my arms. Has my cancer really returned, or is this my imagination? Will I have to face treatments all over again? Will the outcome be favorable this time? When cancer recurs, it can be more serious and advanced. And sometimes it's impossible to treat altogether. Yes, now I am certain my cancer is back. I am sure I'm dying, and this is really real.

Death, we meet again! The idea strikes me hard and fast, like a baseball thrown in the gut. I know the sorry numbers...if my leukemia has relapsed, I don't stand a chance. I try talking myself out of it. *I'm afraid, that's all. Maybe, I could be wrong. But I'm afraid I'm not wrong. I'm afraid I'm right. I'm afraid, I'm afraid, I'm afraid, I'm afraid.* The words keep pounding in my brain like a freight train roaring over the tracks. I am frozen with terror. I can't think, I don't know what to do, and I don't know where to turn.

Joan, you need to calm yourself down. Breathe, I tell myself. *You cannot let other people here see you behave like this; then you'll never get out of this place. You used to be a good actress a long time ago. It must still be in there somewhere. Tap into that part of you, right this very second.*

I haven't scheduled an appointment to talk with you on the phone ahead of time, but I really must talk with you right now. Since we've been working together, I don't recall feeling so desperate that I needed to talk with you immediately. My heart beats hard and fast, like sleet pounding on a window pane. I want to talk to you or see you now. I realize there is a real chance you could firmly say, "No, I'm sorry. You can't have a session with me without scheduling an appointment in advance."

So, what'll it be? Should I call you out of the blue or should I not? Now, one source of panic becomes two. My head is spinning. Is there even time to call you? I cannot waste a precious minute. I know I am crossing the boundary of what's considered acceptable. The fact that I've convinced myself that my symptoms suggest a relapse somewhat borders on the ridiculous, but I'm scared out of my mind. My thoughts keep racing. Joan, get a hold of yourself. Just pick up the phone and call your grief companion. Then again, why bother? You won't pick up the phone. I'll end up crying into an answering machine. Although I feel consumed with humiliation for letting you hear me so panicked and out of control, I must call. I am prepared to be admonished, or worse, flat-out denied a phone session with you. I pray you can tell how desperate I am, and how ashamed I feel to have to beg this way.

Once you bear witness to my level of distress, I imagine you will be glad that I put aside my pride. Perhaps you'd be grateful to know that our trusting bond strengthens each time I expose my vulnerabilities and am met with a kind voice. But most of all, I pray that if you'll just let me talk with you, your special gifts will be waiting — your compassion, wisdom, and loving arms to cradle my fears. You are a beacon of light guiding me in my times of overwhelming despair.

While trying to calm myself down and sort out my miserable thinking, a force in me takes over. Taking a leap of faith, and a huge breath, I dial your office number. I cannot believe my good fortune. No voice recording; for some unknown reason — call it intuition, you miraculously pick up the phone yourself. Deep down, I was praying you would. I take this as a sacred sign. Did you pick up the phone because you knew how much I needed to talk to you, right this very minute? You know it's not like me to plead this way.

I voice my concerns over the phone. If I have relapsed, will I be able to stand strong in my conviction to refuse any more torturous cancer treatments? Can I face the indescribable grief of having to face my own short life coming to an end? Am I ready to die? How can I be sure? In my final days, will I regret not having at least tried a bone marrow transplant, even though I know it involves months of painful inpatient treatment and isolation? Is this really my truth? These are seemingly impossible questions, and I long for your support.

No more diagnostic testing, no more unbearable, invasive treatments, no more physical and mental pain, no more trauma. I have had enough. I am ready to die. I have finally made my decision, this very moment. Privately in the last few months outside our sessions, and in our sessions in between, I rehearse these words again and again. "No more."

HEALING GRIEF

Am I really ready, like I think I am, to accept bringing so much pain to others at my own selfish expense? Do I have the right to die? My decision will cause family and friend's immense suffering, far more lingering than my own. As I near my final months of life, can I be mentally tough enough to face their tears of loss and grief?

There is still a lingering ounce of uncertainty, and now I have no time left to make such a monumental decision about whether or not to treat my cancer recurrence. How can I be completely sure that I'm ready to announce to you and all others, that no matter what, I refuse to go to back to the cancer ward? I refuse to submit to a bone marrow biopsy, the conclusive test that will confirm my relapse once and for all. If the test concludes that my cancer has returned, what will I do? My chances of survival are slim to none according to the statistics. Any days remaining would be filled with immense physical pain. What exactly will I say to loved ones if I make the decision not to have treatment? Let me die now. Let me go. If you love me, you'll forgive me for bringing you heartache and grief.

Is there some protocol about handling fear of recurrence? I am sure my cancer has come back. I am staring straight into its face. I see its blackness, feel my descent towards it. I have never felt this scared. I'm consumed with the same sensation of doom I felt the last time death suddenly came knocking unannounced at my door.

A few months later, my journal entry to my psychotherapist read like this:

Finally! After leaving that awful experience of being hospitalized for depression behind me, I started to slowly, but surely get back to some routine at home. Over a couple of months, as I gained confidence that my cancer would not return and as my depression lifted, I finally started to feel like my old self again. Friends and family had urged me to hang on. They promised that after my anti-depressants finally kicked in, I'd feel better, and they were right!

I feel like I am home free. What a relief. I thought this day would never come. How tremendous it is to be released from what felt like a life in prison. After having survived my grueling cancer treatments and major depression that followed, I am just plain jubilant and feeling lucky to be alive. Wouldn't you be? When I first became depressed eight months ago, I thought it would never come to an end. Now I feel like my immense suffering is finally over! I prayed each day that somehow, some way, I'd one day feel better again. Yet, each long day of misery turned into the next. Living with depression was greater than any dark and gloomy mood imaginable. The greatest burden of depression was the sinking feeling that life could only get worse. I feared I'd have to live out the rest of my days under a dark cloud.

Happiness! Finally! Time for celebration! What can I say, except that it feels so good to feel so good again, just like it felt so depressing to feel so depressed. It's simply a matter of contrasts. The blacker the night, the whiter the stars. The hungrier a person is, the better food tastes. The quieter the morning, the louder birds sing. The more time that goes by without a hug, the better a hug feels. Now that I am back to the land of the living and no longer have to endure prolonged and traumatic treatments, I feel ecstatic.

How could anyone possibly understand the intensity of relief, and how wonderful it is to be alive and feel good again, unless they were standing in my shoes? If they stop to think about it, they probably would feel the very same way. When friends and family suggest I tone my energy level down and try to be less exuberant, I know that they don't understand. They might as well say, "Joan, stop being so happy, will you?"

My husband insists I have lost my sanity, and that I'm not thinking straight. He claims I'm either too high or too low, and that there is a name for this disease. It's called bipolar disorder. He persuades my psychiatrist to go along with the diagnosis, which infuriates me since he relies on Ken's opinion and not mine. Are they trying to say that now I am acting "too gleeful" or "too charged up," and that my elation is truly abnormal?

With a snap of their fingers, they changed their diagnosis from depression to bipolar disorder. Am I actually suffering from a mood disorder called bipolar? I don't think so! In fact, I am sure of it. Pathologic mood swings, they call it. Instead of labeling me "depressed," now they have conveniently come up with a better fit, a different disorder that fits the bill. How I resent that word. Dis-order. It sounds so dis-ease-like.

When will I be able to escape being labeled and stigmatized with one medical diagnosis or another? What will next week's diagnosis bring? What right do they have to attach a label to my degree of happiness? First they observe me, as if I was a caged animal in a science experiment. Then they diagnose my behavior and judge me as if their evaluation is as clear and reliable as performing a physical examination on a patient.

They seem to be obsessed with examining my psyche so they can fit me into one of their nice, neat labels, instead of understanding that their diagnoses are missing the mark. If they survived what I survived, they would also experience a roller coaster, full spectrum of emotions, but ones that were recognizably "normal" given the circumstances.

How could they truly know how wonderful it feels to be alive unless they had walked in my shoes, and unless they had had the experience of looking at death in the face? The fact that I actually survived what I never thought was possible is a complete relief. How could anyone know that feeling of pure joy unless they had gone through what I went through?

Relentless comments about my abrupt mood swings make me feel like I am under constant surveillance. Constantly diagnosing my moods and behavior feels manipulative. Stop scrutinizing me. I am not a lab rat you can simply observe, medicate, lock up, or treat otherwise. Stop trying to fit me into one your convenient labels, when my behaviors, thoughts, and emotions make perfect sense considering the trauma I endured. I am simply human, with no pathology, but with residual trauma, and associated thoughts and behaviors which affect me in ways you simply cannot understand. Bipolar, I am not.

Can't they understand that the more they accuse me of being too happy, or too energized, or too charged up, or too sad or depressed, the more anxious I become? Wouldn't they be annoyed if someone insisted on continually judging their character? Each time family or friends label my behavior, the more furious I become, and the more I insist they get off my back. What right do others have to put a derogatory spin on my happiness?

Once and for all, I've had it with well-intentioned people attempting to control my behavior! I will no longer allow any other person to shame me or insist that I comply with their demands. When friends and family suggest I tone my energy level down or try to be less exuberant, I know they can't possibly understand what I went through. It's as if they are saying, "Joan, stop rejoicing, will you?" Exuberance needn't be pathological or indicative of a form of mental illness. Maybe they're jealous, that's all.

It would make sense that the enthusiasm I feel about being alive, after hovering closely on the verge of death, is commensurate with the degree of suffering I endured. Let's talk about my emotional intensity, as you call it. Others aren't so kind and call my intensity plain annoying. They suggest I work on trying to contain my emotions, to tone down my energy a few notches, as if there were a way I could actually feel things differently. I recognize my energy level is high and can be bothersome to others. I may have the will and desire to calm down for the sake of others, but it's not as if I can program my brain to think or feel with less intensity. Or can I?

When I express myself, I feel limited by the number and degree of descriptive words there are in the English language to reflect the accurate depth or intensity of my feelings. For example, when I describe feeling so sad, so worried, or so lonely, I'm accused of sounding too keyed up and emotional. In my opinion, we just don't have the right words to describe a broader range of emotions.

I wonder if others experience emotions with the same intensity that I do? It doesn't feel like I have conscious control over the way I experience them. My feelings naturally feel the way they do. It's simply how there are. I bet that my heart and head feel things deeply due to my hardwiring. When others stay so emotionally controlled, calm, and rational, I can't help but wonder if life is easier because feelings don't overtake them as forcefully as mine do. When I watch others stay so emotionally calm, their emotional responses often seem dull and not lively enough! Sometimes I want to blurt out, "Feel something, damn it!"

Another journal entry reads:

    My doctor, who insists I have bipolar disorder, now has prescribed lithium, a mood stabilizer I despise. First, I was depressed. Then I was too happy. Now, I'm starting to feel depressed again. Having gained thirty pounds in the last year on lithium, I no longer feel like my feminine, sensual self. Now I feel like a swollen blowfish, a beached whale, a shapeless, sexless, blob. Where did that graceful gazelle go? Gone is the body I worked so hard to maintain, the one I valued and lived in comfortably all these years? I feel foreign, even to myself.

    My interest in sex has vanished. In fact, all my senses are dulled, especially my sense of humor, one of the things I know I need the most. My concentration has fallen away. My brain cannot pay attention to detail, thoughts just don't hang on, and I've lost the ability to find the right words when I speak or when I write. My creativity is gone. When I hear myself speak, my voice sounds shallow, monotone, and weak. My singing is less robust and full.

    My confidence is gone, and I seem to have lost any desire to set new goals or to accomplish much of anything at all. The mood stabilizer the doctors have me on makes me feel so lousy that it feels as if life is not worth living this way. I dream about checking out pretty much every moment of every day. If my doctor won't take my complaints seriously about how lifeless lithium makes me feel and switch me to a different mood stabilizer, then I can't see hanging on to life much longer. One of the hospital psychiatrists, who had the empathy of a cold-blooded shark, threatened, "If you ever take yourself off your medication again, you'll never leave this place...you'll stay here *in this institution for the rest of your life."*

I pose a question to my psychotherapist: "So, you're saying that the only way you'll continue seeing me is if I keep going for regular checkups with my psychiatrist, even though you know how upset I am that he refuses to take me off this medication? You know how many times I have told him that I can't bear staying on lithium one more day, but he's insistent, assuring me that it's the best, most reliable drug to treat bipolar. I have gained more than thirty pounds already and feel like hell."

With lithium, I feel no emotion whatsoever. No happiness, no sadness, no sexual desire, no energy, no nothing. Just plain blah. Nothing gives me a feeling of pleasure, because with this medicine, I can't feel anything. It's like someone gave me a lobotomy, like they cut the "feeling part" of my brain right out. Whenever I complain to my family about how crappy I feel on this medicine, all they say is, "It's a lot better than being depressed." That's easy for them to say.

I can't go on living this way, and if my doctor won't pay attention and switch me to some other medicine, I will find another doctor to go to, no matter what. No one listens to what I have to say. I feel helpless, and I am starting to feel hopeless again. I am so hopeless that I'm being encouraged by my family and doctors to go back into a psychiatric ward. With any luck, maybe the doctors there will be willing to experiment with different medications other than lithium to stabilize my mood. There is one small problem. The only bed available is on a psychiatric unit in a large inner-city hospital. Many of the inmates there are drug addicts, schizophrenic, or psychotic.

A note from my journal when I was re-admitted to the hospital:

I dread this place. I need to let you know what goes on here. It's called solitary confinement. Will this be me? Am I next? I am in my room with my door completely shut, and there is a patient in the room next door screaming and cursing like a maniac at the top of her lungs. I hear her pounding against the wall. Is she pounding with her

HEALING GRIEF

fists, or could it be her head? Am I safe? There is no lock on my door. What if she tries to come in? Then what will I do? She could be violent. She could choke me, even kill me. I am scared out of my mind.

For the first ten minutes, I press my hands tightly against my ears, trying to block out her screams. She must be crying out for someone to help her, and her desperate screams frighten me like a vulnerable child locked in a haunted house. What scares me most is to hear a human being in such pain and distress. The fact that no one comes to ease her suffering makes me realize I am trapped here, too. If no one has come to help her, then who's to say someone would come to my rescue if I was that distressed? No one would come! That's the grim reality. I am completely alone.

Her screams keep me in my hiding place, only because I'm afraid to see what I might become. Maybe this poor woman is having a drug withdrawal, and this is the agony and torture she must bear. Am I destined to live my life in and out of this hellish place forever? What if I keep feeling worse instead of better? Will I become like her? I'd rather die.

I can't bear listening to her screaming one more minute. I need to know what's going on out there. Is she being tortured? I finally can't help myself. After what seems like an hour, I open my door a crack. As I peer out my door, I am horrified to witness two burly security guards who have been summoned to corral her into a corner room, way, way down at the end of the hall. The door of this room looks different than the others. It has a deadbolt.

I watch as one of the guards clasps his hand against his baton. I watch this woman, completely overwrought with terror and grief, being led down the hall in a white straightjacket, her arms tightly crossed against her chest. One guard grabs her on her left side. One grabs her on the right. She is thrashing around, screaming and spitting in their faces. "Get off me, you sons of bitches. I'm going to break your fucking neck. Get your goddamned hands off me." My eyes are not playing tricks on me. This is really happening.

What I see next, I will never be able to erase from my mind. I *watch these two strong men unlock this door and push her in. As the door swings open, I am horrified to see they are locking her in a padded cell. Padded walls, padded floor, padded ceiling. She's screaming louder now, kicking them with her feet, and smashing against them with her shoulders. They slam the door shut, lock the deadbolt, and breathe a deep sigh of relief. They're safe, but is she? Once they shut the door, I can hear her muffled cries, and the sound of her shoulders and head pounding against the door, again and again, desperate to get out.*

The thought of this human being contained and tortured like that makes me sick to my stomach. How can the doctors let this innocent human being suffer this way? What kind of insane place is this? If this woman could lose her mind, then why couldn't I? As humans, we are more alike, than different.

Lessons Learned Ten Years Out

MORE THAN A decade has passed since I was diagnosed with a terminal illness of leukemia at age forty, which began my odyssey in cancer wards and then mental wards as I struggled with depression. How did I actually get better, many people have wanted to know. Where did I muster up that resilience to face one more day? How did I survive what felt like unimaginable loss of control over my life?

As I reflect back over the two major parts of my story, my first twelve months of grueling medical treatments for leukemia, and then my two-year battle with depression, it's challenging to try to fit all of the pieces neatly together to figure out how exactly I managed to get through this ordeal. When did things start to fall apart, and when did they finally start coming together again? What went wrong and how? What worked to help me put my life back together again? These were questions worth thinking about, and they evoked lessons to be learned that no one could teach me but myself.

As a prelude to this chapter titled, "Lessons Learned," I want to point out that I condensed the majority of the transformative work that took place during the course of psychotherapy. It might seem somewhat perplexing how I seemed to have gotten well so quickly. The fact is, the process of doing the work of therapy was laborious, and it often felt like I was taking one step forward and two steps back.

Nature took its course, and life began to blossom again, as I gradually resumed my busy schedule with a fresh, new start. The old me—the one before these catastrophic events—faded into the backdrop as time went by. At the same time, the "new me" emerged, fortified and richer because of having gone through hell and gotten to the other side. Looking back, it took a good two-and-a-half years after being diagnosed with leukemia and then a major depression until I began to feel more secure and confident in the "new me." With time, my depression completely vanished, and my leukemia stayed in remission beyond the five-year-survival medical milestone. I was home free.

That is, until breast cancer appeared out of the blue seven years later. I hadn't noticed any symptoms at all. This time around, just as I had learned from having faced leukemia and a major depression, battling a disease would not have a nice, neat start and finish. If I was unlucky, I might not reach the finish line at all. There would be twists and turns and obstacles to face. I didn't know where my journey would end up taking me, and that all-too-familiar roller coaster of emotions cropped up again. I was hoping luck would be in my favor since my breast cancer was found early. My gynecologist took notice of it at an annual checkup even before I did. "Here, I want you to feel something," she said, as she took my fingertips and led them to the exact spot in my left breast until I could feel a tiny pencil eraser-size bump underneath the skin. Here we go again, I thought instantly.

This time felt different immediately, since I approached this second cancer with the success of having endured hardship before. I knew I had what it took to overcome this catastrophic brush with death at a young age because I had proven to myself before that I could do it. With a new inner strength that had developed from surviving the last set of terrifying, life-threatening illnesses, I knew I could get through this, too. I was now more confident in my abilities, having had years behind me to fine-tune many of the coping strategies I had learned along the way.

Describing in detail the specific steps I took along my breast cancer journey would require a separate memoir. In summary, difficult surgical treatment decisions resulted in a mastectomy, then four subsequent reconstruction surgeries over the next five-year period. I also needed adjuvant hormonal therapy, which was accompanied by unpleasant side effects, and these became the new set of challenges I needed to face. I still fantasize about the possibility of the girls having a "matched set" one day, an expression used by my breast cancer oncologist when she told me about the surgical and tattoo techniques to make aesthetic corrections after breast cancer. However, I think I need to take a break from surgery just a little while longer.

The question becomes, how much longer is a "little while," and do I have a "little while longer" left to live? This question has become my True North, the needle on my inner compass that guides me on my journey, for as many days as I have left to live. I hope I have many! There's so much left to do. Spending joyful time with family and friends, celebrating marriage and commitment ceremonies, having fun with grandchildren one day, seizing new opportunities to travel, continuing to do work in my chosen profession, and relaxing and having fun along the way. Each year now as new birthdays roll around, I am grateful for my life in a way I never knew existed. Every new day is an unexpected birthday gift.

That familiar gold standard of being "cured" arrived for the second time in my life—five years in the clear post-cancer. With each passing day, three consecutive traumas—first leukemia, then a long period of major depression, followed by breast cancer—increasingly feel over time like an historic blip on my medical radar screen.

But how did I find my way through this confusing maze? First, I had to get the facts straight, as learning empowered me to understand my illnesses and understand their trajectory along a continuum. What's happening to my body now, and what will happen to it in the future? What can I expect along the way? How do I get from Point A to Point B? What don't I understand, and where can I go to get answers? How can I make difficult treatment decisions?

In my case, I learned everything I could about managing my treatments by reading anything I could get my hands on—academic, nonfiction and fiction books, journals and memoirs, and by gathering information on the internet and from other survivors. Each person's cancer journey, mental health journey, and ways to cope are unique, but for me, I cannot overstate how helpful reading and research became. There are many excellent resource materials available for people facing a life-threatening illness, as well as for their families.

Although unconventional to do so in a personal memoir, I am so thankful for the insight and understanding I gained from the materials I found and refer back to again and again, that I've created a resource list at the end of this book. I hope these references will be beneficial and offer you the same sense of personal empowerment and wisdom that they provided me.

When people receive a diagnosis of cancer or other life-threatening illness, the first thing that comes to mind is whether they will survive. Concern at that immediate point is somatic in nature. Can my body physically be healed by treatment, or will my body not be able to withstand the treatments, and will I die from that, or from other complications of the illness? Other parts of the body, all of equal importance, also need care and tending to, as cancer affects a person's whole being—psychological, cognitive, behavioral, social, and spiritual.

My Experience With the Mental Health System

DEPRESSION IS STILL often an unspoken topic for a person facing a life-threatening illness because of the stigma involved. Drs. Jeremy Winell, MD and Andrew J. Roth, MD capture the question clearly in their research on depression in cancer patients. "If you had cancer, wouldn't you feel depressed too?" Their research shows that up to 17% of terminally ill cancer patients have expressed a desire for hastened death.

Dr. Jimmie Holland, MD, who pioneered the psycho-oncology field, asserts that physical and psychological distress are closely related, and that one-third to one-half of all women will experience psychological distress after a cancer diagnosis, throughout treatment, and beyond. Years of research show that emotional distress is normal, and that cancer is typically associated with fatigue, vulnerability, uncertainty, helplessness, social isolation, fear of recurrence, sexuality concerns, anxiety and depression.

At the time of my depression, I tried learning all I could to try to make sense of why I was so deeply affected from the trauma and side effects associated with my treatments, when it seemed like others, in comparison, seemed to psychologically sail through theirs. While I was still trying to sort things out, I learned about Dr. Jimmie Holland from Ken's *Oncology Times* newsletter. I felt that finally I had found someone who understood me and who recognized that treating a person facing cancer requires a multi-dimensional approach. It was such a relief and validation to learn about her tireless dedication to educate other members of the medical community about the distress cancer patients and their families face, and how vital it is to address and treat the accompanying psychosocial stress, as well.

Never in my life had I been depressed or manic before being diagnosed and treated for leukemia. This fact underscored the validity of why I knew it wasn't simply genetic, or that it could be eliminated with "the right pill." Rather, I knew in my heart that it was directly connected to the circumstances surrounding my crisis.

Joseph Campbell, a prolific writer, lecturer, and mythologist, wrote about the significant value of suffering, saying that depression is like a natural death or a "healthy" closing down of the body and mind for useful, adaptive reasons. This internal shutting down is a far safer alternative to, for example, suicide. In effect, Campbell says that during a depression, life gets put on hold for a while. In a way, people take a mental "break" until circumstances change which support their re-entry into life.

While I was taking this mental "break" from life, I was continuously frustrated and resentful that it seemed as though my doctor's desire was to fit me into a nice, neat tidy box labeled "Mental Illness." The stigma of being diagnosed as mentally ill, and the process of labeling me depressed one day, and bipolar the next, made me feel worse. It compounded my sense of hopelessness. I already had enough to cope with emotionally at the time, and I was busy struggling to figure out the reason why I was "the only one I knew" who became depressed. Then again, I knew no one else in my circumstances. If only I had been a "better, stronger survivor" throughout my treatments, then I wouldn't have fallen apart mentally and emotionally, I reprimanded myself.

A couple of years after I stopped seeing my psychiatrist for regular appointments, I went back for a visit to say hello. He confided that he had recently heard of similar cases like mine, and that he now had a better understanding of how the massive doses of steroids which I

HEALING GRIEF

needed to take in order to survive my cancer treatments had caused a temporary chemical imbalance in the brain, a specific condition called steroid-induced bipolar.

Instead of simply treating the depression with a magic pill, what needed to be addressed and treated was the underlying cause of my depression, which was both biological in origin and deeply informed by post-traumatic stress. I told my doctor that I felt his insistence on this initial diagnosis of bipolar disorder was demoralizing, unhelpful, and inappropriate given the massive amounts of steroids I was administered to clear my multiple infections. He listened carefully, took a deep breath, and explained that doctors now have a much better understanding of how high-dose steroid administration produces mood symptoms that mimic the ups and downs of true bipolar disorder.

What about the people in my life who accused me of being too upbeat, and too intense at times, specifically during the time period following my recovery from depression? Why was I so high on life? Clinical psychologist and bipolar disorder expert, Kay Redfield Jamison, PhD, explains that "exuberance" does not always indicate pathological mania, but that instead, it represents a vital "irrepressible life force" in all of us. According to this view on bipolar disorder, I wasn't pathologically manic after all.

In retrospect, and with respect to my psychiatrist and others who suspected I had developed bipolar disorder, I can see how they arrived at that conclusion, which as I have mentioned, infuriated me at the time. The healing process was not at all linear, and admittedly, my moods vacillated significantly following my cancer treatments. As a backdrop to my cancer and depression, significant highs and lows occurred in the life of our budding young family. The set of life circumstances that arose during this time period would throw just about any person off-track for a while. After feeling so vulnerable and unsteady after my cancer treatments and periods of depression, these events had an even greater impact on me, particularly because I didn't think I would live long enough to see them. Because of their intensity, my various moods—excited, fearful, grieving, ashamed, elated—could have easily been misconstrued as symptoms of bipolar disorder.

It was a psychological high to be declared officially in remission by my oncologist after my first round of treatment. Did this mean I was cured? When it comes to cancer, medical professionals are hesitant to use the word "cure" because the honest-to-goodness fact is that, statistically, one can never be sure that cancer won't return. Additionally, it felt tremendous to be alive and well enough to attend one wonderful celebration after another with family and friends after making it through Round One of my cancer treatments. We were so elated that we took our children to a deluxe family resort, something we would never have treated ourselves to "before cancer." It was a vacation I had always wanted to go on, and here, I finally had the chance. That felt great.

I got my very first cell phone, so I could stay in touch with family and friends while at the hospital, which felt luxurious at the time. Ask any teenager and they'll tell you how exciting that is for them, too. Becoming a cancer survivor even became my ticket to owning a new car. I had desperately needed a new set of wheels before being diagnosed with leukemia, because the ten-year-old clunker that I had been driving was unreliable and on its last legs, just like me. Honestly, I would have been glad to receive the gift of a brand new bike, as a hopeful reminder that I would soon grow strong enough to ride again one day. When Ken surprised me with car keys, I felt like a movie star. What a high!

I got very attached to this new car of mine. I treated it with love and drove it for ten years thereafter, never wanting to give it away, since it was symbolic of getting through my treatments and still being alive, after literally staring at death in the face. In fact, when it was time to sell this beloved car of mine and turn my keys over to the auto salesman, I began to cry, which was completely embarrassing, mind you. It was at that precise moment that the previous feeling of utter joy and relief from *not dying* flooded through me. The salesman was a grief counselor at heart. He offered me a tissue from his desk and emphatically reassured me that I was definitely not the only car

HEALING GRIEF

owner who had done the very same thing.

Furthermore, it was also exhilarating to still be alive to witness our oldest daughter graduate high school, especially after being certain that I would not live long enough to see her reach this milestone. It felt great, really great, to be healthy enough to take her to look at different colleges. This involved arranging elaborate travel plans and setting up multiple interviews and appointments. I started to believe in myself again after realizing my organizational skills weren't as rusty as I had thought.

In contrast, it was a major loss and psychological low point when the graduation ceremony was over, and it was time to send her off to college. Understandably, this was a major loss because my professional life had been centered around helping deaf and hard of hearing youth and families. What could measure up to the joys and challenges of teaching about deafness and disabilities at a local college, or writing books and speaking internationally on the topic of educating children who are deaf and hard of hearing in the mainstream, or advocating to create laws to provide captions in public places like schools and movie theaters? I developed a social support group for deaf and hard of hearing teenagers and took a leadership role with school professionals and families united in addressing children's and families' needs around deafness. Given that, imagine the magnitude of loss when my own daughter left the nest. It felt like a major chapter in my life had suddenly come to an abrupt end.

Another major low point was attending our middle daughter's Bat Mitzvah when I was at the height of one of my depressive periods. Although I was physically well enough to attend—only with my mother's insistence and her pulling me out of bed, getting me dressed, and doing my hair and makeup—I felt down-right miserable. Though this should have been a happy, uplifting occasion, I knew in my heart that I had done a poor job helping my daughter get ready to face this milestone. I was on lithium at the time of her special event, so instead of feeling happy like I should have felt, I was feeling out-of-it. If I wasn't feeling depressed enough already, living with the shame of not being a better mother made me feel even worse. My mood suffered and down I fell.

I had been in a state of great anxiety anyway, feeling like I was being forced to relocate to Connecticut the minute our first child left home to go to college. I was already feeling sad enough from the aftermath of "losing" our oldest child and experiencing the so-called "empty nest syndrome" for the first time. And now on top of that loss, I was anticipating yet another huge loss of having to say goodbye to friends and colleagues, as well as my side of the family who lived nearby. They were my supporters, and the idea of leaving them behind felt painfully sad.

And yet, despite these losses, it was also a psychological high just being able to get back to being a wife and a hands-on mom for our younger two children who were still in the nest, and who had not been able to lean on me as much as I would have liked during my illnesses. In sum, so many significant changes in the life of my family, some happy and some sad, hit me all at once. Miraculously, time was now on my side. And with that luxury, the highs and lows eventually settled into a new normal.

The prominent psychiatrist, Dr. Thomas Szasz, spent his life-long career advocating for the rights of psychiatric patients. His work and principles gave me hope and helped me to believe in myself again. In his years of research, he found that while mental patients continue to be physically restrained, they are also "restrained chemically." Szasz explains that the field of psychiatry and our mental health system's fundamental purpose is to create two classes of people—those who are stigmatized as mentally ill and subjected to coercive psychiatric intervention, and then the ones who are left behind, the "normal" ones whom he calls "unmolested." Molested may sound like a strong term, yet, that is how I felt, stolen away from my home and family, robbed of freedom to make my own choices and decisions, and forced to live behind locked doors.

A survival tactic that provided me the most comfort in the hospital was to temporarily disassociate myself through journaling. This became my main tool to escape from the man banging his head against the floor and the woman in the straightjacket being dragged into the isolation room. It was both laughable and infuriating when I met with the on-call psychiatrist for a mandatory weekly session, and he started by saying, "So I understand you have been engaging in excessive writing behavior."

Like Szasz describes, the mental health system is fraught with dynamics that unfortunately dehumanize, humiliate, and misrepresent the various tools people use to cope with psychic suffering. Andrew Solomon, MD, a psychiatrist who writes about his own personal experiences with depression asserts that an institution can be the worst possible place to send a depressed person, and yet, that was where I was ultimately sent as a last resort.

Importance of Finding a Grief Companion

FROM THE MOMENT a person is given a life-threatening diagnosis, counseling and mental health services should be offered and encouraged. Prior to embarking on stressful treatments, patients should be educated by a member of their healthcare team about the possibility of depression, as well as about prevention and treatment strategies. Otherwise, scores of cancer patients and those facing other life-threatening illnesses are bound to face depression and suicidal ideation or attempts. Without psychological support and guidance, a patient's psychic energy, very much needed to overcome the physical toll of cancer treatments, can come crashing down. At this point, little or nothing is left in reserve to manage the accompanying psychological, emotional, and spiritual challenges they face.

The longer depression continues, the harder it is to treat. Patients often cover up feelings of depression for fear of embarrassment and shame, or worry that they will become a greater burden or be misunderstood by family and friends. No matter how lousy depression makes a patient feel, the fear and unpleasantness of opening up to someone can seem worse. Patients typically fear that they would be admitting failure if they reach out for help. The thought of revealing feelings of isolation, hopelessness, or fear that they might be going crazy altogether, can often prohibit people with depression from having faith and courage to step forward and talk about it.

◄ **HEALING GRIEF**

After all, it seems as if no other patients except for themselves seem to be depressed, which makes sense since other patients don't talk about their depression either. Rather than opening Pandora's Box and facing the fear of mental illness, it's easier to continue hoping and praying that feelings of depression will disappear naturally over time. Sometimes, in fact, this is the case, and once patients finish treatments and begin to get well, their depression naturally subsides. But as child psychologist Bruno Bettleheim explains, for other cancer patients with depression, what can't be talked about can't be cured.

A person like me who was experiencing PTSD, finds it impossibly painful to put thoughts and feelings into words. Doing so is terrifying; it's like re-living the same harrowing experiences all over again. Each time, sensory feelings take over which interfere with the part of the brain that helps put thoughts into words. Flashbacks, which are miserable if you've never experienced them, are one of several symptoms that distinguish "normal grief" from post-traumatic stress disorder.

From what I've researched and learned, facing a tragic or catastrophic event stirs up feelings that we may not be aware of, but that continually simmer underneath the surface. All we know is how hard it is to face them or give voice to them, especially when they have had time to build up inside. It seems easier not to think about them, let alone talk about them.

Terry L. Wise, public speaker and author, bravely shares her personal demons and triumphs as a suicide survivor. As the primary caregiver of her young husband battling Lou Gehrig's disease (ALS), Terry did a heroic job keeping a stiff upper lip. She chose not to talk to anyone about the impact her husband's disease was having on her mental health. She didn't want to be seen as a complainer, and she thought it was the smart and brave thing to do to keep her feelings zipped up inside. Her website and book contain sage advice on how to prevent depression and suicide by doing what feels most difficult at the time, that is, talking about difficult emotions so they don't continually escalate. Terry ultimately discovered that talking about painful feelings helps because it releases the pain.

IMPORTANCE OF FINDING A GRIEF COMPANION

In addition to voicing feelings, taking mental breaks from grief can also be healthy. Research has shown that young children in particular, naturally take healthy grief breaks. Many children experience what Alan Wolfelt, PhD, thanatologist and head of the Center for Loss and Life Transition calls "grief-bursts," when they will suddenly start sobbing one minute, then head off to the playground the next minute. It seems as if they're able to turn their grief emotions off and on with a simple flick of a switch. Studies show that, compared to adults, grieving children can more easily mask their pain. The grief is there all right, but to the outside world, it looks invisible.

Studies show that adults grieve differently, more often in a concentrated, prolonged way. Emotional pain from grief and loss feels dismal, and it is hard to give voice to for people of all ages. Chronic worry and hopelessness is the norm, not the exception. "My life feels out of control. I feel completely lost." If painful, dark emotions such as these aren't expressed in healthy ways, they escalate, and express themselves in unhealthy, destructive ways. Inability to concentrate, nightmares, sleeplessness, eating disorders, street drugs or alcohol, depression, and even suicide are known consequences of unresolved grief.

I was no different. As my feelings continued to build inside, it got to the point where I didn't want to talk about them either. I had convinced myself that talking about them would make me feel worse, not better. And I was feeling bad enough. I stopped talking and kept my fears to myself. They began to snowball and with each day, they grew so big and ominous that I became too scared to talk about them.

Why didn't I just open and spill the beans with the hope of feeling relief afterwards? Trauma can have immense psychosocial consequences. When confronted with a threat to their physical integrity, people experience post-traumatic stress that is often masked by symptoms of depression. It often feels and looks the same, not only to others but to one's self. Feelings and symptoms commonly associated with post-traumatic stress disorder (PTSD) can also often look on the surface like depression and mental illness. Expressing thoughts and feelings is hard and unpleasant, but it helps a grieving person eventually move beyond the pain of loss.

Seeing a professional counselor or faith leader is not necessary for everyone, but it was my salvation. I don't think I could have lived without it. With the help of a gifted psychotherapist, personal growth and renewal was possible. My psychotherapist's office became the cozy haven where I could be myself without fear of judgment or shame and without worry about hearing ridiculing statements like, "If I were you, I would have gotten over this by now," or "How could you feel like giving up…you can't really mean that, could you? I wish you wouldn't talk that way." My psychotherapist, on the other hand, was an open slate. She helped brush those "could've, would've, should've's" aside and let me explore how to work things out on my own, knowing that way, they would have sticking power.

Although "talk therapy" is a vital first step when creating a coping toolbox, medication can have a beneficial place, too. I knew that finding the right selective serotonin reuptake inhibitors (SSRIs), the most common anti-anxiety and depression medications, could successfully alter my brain chemistry that had gone out of whack, but also couldn't make my depression disappear completely on its own. SSRIs can help treat depression, but they often cause such unpleasant side effects that patients often prefer not to take medication. All SSRIs have the potential to incite akathisia, or restlessness which I've described previously as spiders crawling up one's spine, in already distressed patients. This subsequently increases suicide risk as patients will do anything, including end their lives, in order to cease the discomfort.

What I needed most was continuous supportive care by a trained professional from the moment of diagnosis with a terminal illness. Through his work as a hematologist-oncologist and his family experience with cancer, Dr. Kenneth D. Miller, MD, my husband, has become a leading international expert on cancer survivorship. He asserts that someone is a cancer survivor from the moment of diagnosis, and that supportive care should be provided throughout the process of diagnosis, treatment, and long-term recovery.

IMPORTANCE OF FINDING A GRIEF COMPANION ➤

What if I had been encouraged from the start to give voice to my intense spectrum of thoughts and feelings, and to share, not hide, the multiple traumatic incidences I confronted? What if I had received reassurance and validation from the start and all along the way that my complex feelings were neither good or bad, nor right or wrong, but that it was important to my mental health to speak the truth?

There are research studies that conclude that depression and PTSD can be prevented if there are safety nets in place, such as a person whose role it is to accompany a patient at every step of his or her journey. As human beings, we are hardwired for connection, a biological process called "limbic regulation" in which we positively influence one another's central nervous systems. As a result, patients who are hospitalized for long stretches of time can feel particularly isolated without the support of others. The role of a grief counselor is not to "fix" the patient's grief, but rather to serve as a trustworthy companion and confidante. With this type of support, those facing a crisis would have a safe environment available to begin to identify, understand, and integrate feelings, and ultimately make peace with them.

Building on the early work of Dr. Jimmie Holland, MD, research continues on the psychosocial implications of cancer. Fortunately, we now have whole ranks of healthcare professionals and researchers diligent about finding optimal ways to treat patients facing a life-threatening illness. In the field of cancer treatment, it has been a continual challenge, often an uphill battle, to enlighten physicians and their medical teams about how necessary psychosocial support is as a means of preventing psychological distress and mental illness.

During those early years of my cancer diagnosis, the field of psycho-oncology was only just gaining momentum. That meant for our family, we needed to do a lot of scrambling around, trying to piece together which services were available, if any, and that created additional stress we needed to manage. Since that time, the field of traumatology has burgeoned, beginning with the early work of Dr. Bessel van der Kolk, who explored trauma through brain imaging studies. We need to continue to reform the current paradigm of mental health research and, in particular, allocate funding and concentrate new research on the benefits of psychosocial support from "Day One of Diagnosis" to prevent depression and suicide in patients suffering with long-term physical illness.

A grief counselor is essential, a safe someone who is non-judgmental with no hidden agenda. Their entire goal is to companion the bereaved, and they can be in the form of any safe, trustworthy person, such as a professional mental health counselor or another member of one's healthcare team. Grief counseling can also be in the form of a small or large in-person support group. Some people thrive by taking part in large survivor advocacy efforts and fundraising groups, such as Susan G. Komen for the Cure, Leukemia and Lymphoma Society, or National Alliance on Mental Illness. These support services help people to overcome feelings of isolation and existential loneliness during trying times.

What I learned is that the importance of reaching out to a grief companion can't be overestimated. It is essential, especially if you feel like you are becoming depressed or suicidal. A caring, listening presence is what I needed most, especially in my darkest moments. I desperately needed someone "on my team." Judgmental phrases from others such as, "Don't talk that way," or "How can you think like that?" pushed me deeper into depression. For then, not only was I suffering, but I was also feeling misunderstood.

Why is a grief companion so precious and invaluable? It is someone willing to bear witness, to journey along as a companion, to validate and provide an emotional safety net, and to offer hope and provide faith. The magic of a grief companion is that the relationship provides a safe sanctuary for patients to unburden their souls. Inside this sanctuary, there is room for tears of sadness, fright, anger, or regret. A grief companion is that noble soul who comes with no agenda other than to listen, be attentive, and acknowledge another person's private suffering.

To be known by another, especially in the depths of personal despair, lifts the burden of vulnerability, guilt, shame, and loneliness.

IMPORTANCE OF FINDING A GRIEF COMPANION

With full permission to disclose one's true feelings, a grieving person is reassured that someone will still be willing to stand by their side. A grief companion provides a bereaved person safety, support, and encouragement to believe in their newly emerging self.

What I needed early on, from the onset of my diagnosis, but didn't get, was a consistent, professional grief companion and patient advocate. I can't help but wonder if I had had a "bereavement facilitator" or "grief companion" on an ongoing, steady basis to validate my feelings of anxiety, terror, and isolation, then perhaps my post-traumatic stress in the form of major depression could have been prevented. Even just a brief visit with a fantastic social worker, Matt Loscalzo, taught me to focus on my breath, moment by moment, to work through the pain of cancer treatments. He helped calm my fears by creating a mantra: "This too shall pass." Matthew Loscalzo, MSW, Director of Supportive Care Medicine at City of Hope, has been a crusader in promoting the screening and treatment of distress in cancer survivors, and he teaches healthcare professionals to pay attention to psychosocial barriers in the treatment of patients with life-threatening illnesses.

During my treatment, I also met a clinical psychologist, Dr. R. Patrick Savage, past president of the Maryland Psychological Association, who taught me about the usefulness of guided imagery and visualization. Listening to guided imagery audiotapes—in particular, visualizing a sailboat gliding along crystal blue-green water—became a transformative coping tool that helped me overcome physical, mental, and emotional pain. These meetings were incredibly helpful, and I could have benefited from even more consistent "companionship" by a mental health provider.

Later in my therapy work, I was encouraged to experiment with a repertoire of evidence-based tools for pain and stress management that I wish I could have started practicing immediately at the time of diagnosis. I longed to have a reassuring, non-judgmental person with no agenda of their own to hear me out and validate my experience, help me maintain hope for the future, and rebuild my ego strength.

◄ **HEALING GRIEF**

This was what I needed most at the time of diagnosis but did not get enough of from my medical team.

The expression goes that when the student is ready, the teacher appears. After trying out different therapists and continually searching for a comfortable fit, I felt blessed to have an exceptional therapist come into my life. Although our therapy sessions were tearful and felt messy and uncomfortable much of the time, I felt better afterwards. I learned that it was not only okay, but that it was great to have a good cry. Research shows that tears can flush negative chemicals out of the body. Clarissa Pinkola Estés, an internationally-recognized scholar, poet, and Jungian psychoanalyst writes about the transformative nature of tears.

Grateful beyond words, I appreciated finally finding a compassionate grief companion who offered a safe place where all of my feelings, no matter how extreme, were validated and understood. There was so much to grieve because there was so much loss: loss of health, vitality, and close connections with colleagues, family, and friends. With her relentless, steady support, I eventually recovered.

Assembling a Coping Toolbox

I NEEDED TO develop a personal list of coping strategies to help manage physical pain and other physical symptoms such as nausea, vomiting, and fatigue. Separately, I needed a toolbox of coping strategies to manage complex feelings: fear, anger, sorrow, guilt, shame, confusion, and depression.

Just around the time I was nearing the end of my third inpatient cancer treatment cycle, it felt like the effects of the chemotherapy in my body went from bad to worse, and my mental and emotional health took a nosedive along with it. Over the years, I tried to live by the credo that when lemons appear, try making lemonade. Although I was thirsty to figure out how to accomplish this, there seemed to be little movement in a positive direction.

During my illnesses and times in between, some of the coping cools I used were unhealthy, maladaptive ones. I wouldn't recommend them: sleeping for hours during the day, drinking too much alcohol, taking addictive anxiety medication such as Ativan or Valium. These strategies felt great at the time. They were effective in masking emotional pain and gave me the quick-fix I was looking for, because they instantly made me feel better. However, their effectiveness was temporary, and as soon as the good feeling wore off within a couple of hours, I returned to an ever lower place than before.

The grieving and healing process is unique for each person, and there's truly no way to know what someone's favorite tools will be until they're tried on for size. I can only share the tools that best helped me, and still help me as I look ahead, knowing that a disaster can strike at any time. None of us is immune. Nonetheless, you may be wondering what helped me get through, and how I personally managed to handle the entire gestalt, the collection of body-mind-spiritual challenges that accompanied my physical treatments.

It was amazing to discover that the more I practiced, the easier and more useful they became, to the point where I no longer had to think about doing them. Like learning to ride a bike, they kicked in automatically. I am many years beyond cancer, and I still rely on many of these same strategies to handle the ordinary stress and strain in life.

Here is just a short list of coping tools that continue to serve me along this journey:

Knowledge and self-awareness through education. Support from family, friends, community, and clergy or faith leaders. Hope. Prayer. Faith. Individual and group counseling. Psychosocial support groups (in person or online). Grief support online chatrooms and blogs. Expressive arts, including journaling, reading, writing, drawing, painting, music, dance, and sandplay. Exercise. Swimming. Drumming. Singing. Enjoying concerts. Exploring the outdoors. Nature walks. Gardening. Visiting a park, arboretum, or museum. Giving hugs. Getting hugs. Crying. Laughing. Watching a funny film. Reading a funny story or a book of jokes or riddles. Cozying up with a teddy bear, a beloved pet, or infant. Volunteering to help others. Telling your story and listening to others tell theirs. Reaching out to someone less fortunate. Reciting "This too shall pass." Taking multi-vitamins. Trying out different anti-depressants until you find one that works. Cooking organic foods. Mindfulness and meditation. Guided Imagery. Acupuncture. Massage. Reiki. Craniosacral therapy. Yoga. The list goes on.

Journaling

JOURNALING WAS AN expressive art form that helped me from beginning to end. It became one of the most helpful coping tools throughout my journey. Because it was so painful to talk about my feelings freely, I began to write instead. Journaling gave me a safe place to let my feelings out. It was what helped me to move forward and to get through what felt like insurmountable obstacles, especially during my depression.

I needed someone or something to lean on, and writing became that "something" I relied on until I could stand on my own two feet again. Paper and pencil followed me everywhere I went. Some of my most productive writing and expression of intensely painful thoughts and feelings occurred in the late night hours when the house was peaceful and quiet. In the mornings, as well, in that moment between sleep and wakefulness, my thoughts would crystallize into words that I'd record in my journal.

In recent years, over two hundred studies about trauma survivors show that writing a trauma narrative is a healthy psychological mechanism to ward off depression and anxiety. Writing helps survivors coalesce various traumatic experiences into a storytelling framework that connects meaning to their suffering and helps them transcend grief.

Thoughts and feelings flowed through me, from heart and soul to pen and paper. Putting my emotions into words helped me get better in touch with how I was feeling inside. Writing released my pent-up feelings, and I knew that I'd always feel better afterwards, no matter how hard it was to do. Through the process of journaling, I was able to explore, deeply and at a comfortable pace, many of the existential issues with which I was struggling—the meaning and value of time, life, love, intimacy, spirituality, death and dying, grief and loss, suffering, and transcendence.

Journaling can be your own personal grief companion. It's a gift you can give yourself to help you move through the grieving process. You have the freedom to write exactly what you want. It's meant for your eyes only, unless you choose to share your thoughts and feelings with someone else. The benefit of keeping a journal is that it's both portable and private. You have total freedom to express yourself however you wish. There are no right or wrong feelings. They are *your* feelings, and through journaling, you create a safe place to acknowledge and to work through them at your own pace.

Close your eyes for a minute or two. Let your mind go and see which thoughts rise to the top. Don't overthink, or try to talk yourself out of writing the thought that first pops into your mind. Go ahead and write that one thought down. That's a fine start. These singular thoughts and feelings are grist for the mill. They become a vital part of the grieving process, necessary for healing. Ignore the temptation or worry to fix spelling or punctuation errors. That will interrupt your thought process and slow you down.

Let as many feelings as possible rise to the surface. Or, consider creating a list of positive and negative thoughts and feelings. Maybe a short phrase will pop into your mind, or a list, or poem. Write it all down. Or try putting your thoughts and feelings into a sentence, starting with words like Anger. Sadness. Worry. Regret. Fear. Hopeless. Happy. Relieved. Hopeful.

Consider writing a letter, which eventually you can choose to share with that person, or choose not to share, in which case, rip it up and throw it away. "Dear So and So….What I wish I could say to you is…," or "Thank you for…," or "The people I can depend most on are…," or "What I can do to help myself get through this hard time is…."

JOURNALING

What you choose to write is for your eyes only, unless you choose to share it. That's quite empowering at a time in life when so much feels out of control, and when rules are dictated by others. With journaling, you are in total control. Writing keeps *you* in change. A journal is a safe place where no one judges your thoughts and feelings, criticizes you, or tells you how you should or should not feel.

Over the years, family, friends and colleagues remark, "I wish I could be a writer like you. I could never do that. I wouldn't know where to start." Generally I reply, "Sure you could. Don't think about grammar and punctuation. Don't judge yourself."

The beauty of journaling or letter writing is that you can release your pent-up emotions, unload the burden you're carrying, and free up your spirit, at a time when thoughts and feelings are too difficult to talk about face to face. There's not much to it, other than the hardest part, which requires taking the first step of picking up a pen.

Heroes and Role Models

AS I COMPARED my cancer story to others, it was important for me to figure out why I felt I didn't have what it took to mentally and emotionally handle the rigorous treatments and side effects. If others could, why couldn't I? Over time, I have come to realize that the type of cancer and degree of physical pain involved differs for each survivor. In my case of acute myelogenous leukemia, the physical, bone-crunching, sword-in-the-back type of pain was profound and often impossible to stay on top of, even with the maximum dose of IV morphine. This degree of physical pain overwhelmed my psyche. I'm sure that my accompanying sense of terror and impending annihilation felt like an exaggeration to some family and friends, but for me, it felt impossible to shake. Life seemed to scream danger.

One of my dearest friends for over thirty-five years has been suffering with multiple sclerosis that has advanced to where she can no longer walk, take care of her bodily needs without help, or even feed herself on days where the muscles in her hands give out. If she can still keep her eyes on the future, then couldn't I? If Nick Vujicic, motivational speaker, born without arms and legs, can embrace each day with pride and dignity, then couldn't I? If dozens of "ordinary people" whose memoirs I read could overcome challenges of epic proportion, couldn't I learn from their experiences? And if these ordinary people were brave enough to write their stories in the hope that they might inspire others, well...couldn't I try, too?

I love to read narratives written by survivors that have come before me to help lead the way. These heroes inspire me and provide hope, as they courageously share their own personal stories of overcoming challenges. Equally courageous as the heroes I read about in books were the dedicated friends, family, and neighbors who graciously stepped in and did whatever was possible to help our family when we were in distress. They gave me strength and inspiration to carry on, especially on days when I thought I was unable to take one more step.

Mindfulness and Spirituality

WE KNOW THAT each person faces grief and loss, and hope and healing differently, and this applies to the spiritual dimension of their being as well. Elisabeth Kübler-Ross, MD, a pioneer in the field of death and dying, introduced me to the notion that facing one's mortality directly, much like a head-on collision, can open a person to the spiritual part of their being. But what about me? How could that possibly happen, I wondered? I had no "religious" or "spiritual part" per se, or, at least none that I was aware of.

All I knew with certainty was that I had been an atheist since I was a teenager. The conclusion I had arrived at decades before was that religious faith was a bad thing. There was no scientific proof that it had value, and all I could clearly see was that it tore groups of people apart and caused thousands of years of antagonism and destruction.

Some grievers become furious and question how God or a higher spirit could have let such a catastrophe happen. They feel lost and turn away with a sense of betrayal and disappointment, never looking back. Others turn to organized religion or faith-based groups for the first time, appreciating the miracle of having lived and gotten a second chance. Surviving cancer made me start to wonder if there was, in fact, a higher power or a source of concentrated atoms and electrons orchestrating what was going on down here on earth.

I began to wonder if perhaps it wasn't a sheer coincidence after all that I became well at the exact same time that hundreds of people were reassuring me that they were sending prayers of faith and

MINDFULNESS AND SPIRITUALITY

healing energy my way. I conjured up a mental image of the energy in the cells of all those people swirling together to create one massive force. That was a whole lot of healing energy, and I decided that prayer, even though it is invisible, must have a positive value. The "old me," before cancer and depression would have said, "Hogwash!" The "new me" is the first one to say with genuine sincerity to a friend in ill-health, "I will be sending prayers your way."

As I continued questioning the possibility of opening up the spiritual part of myself, as usual, I started looking to role models and heroes to lead the way. If the Dalai Lama could win a Nobel Peace Prize, I decided I should investigate meditation and hopeful prayer for peace and good health, like he does. There must be something to it. With a great deal of practice, I discovered the tranquil benefits of mindfulness and meditation.

After reading the work of Jon Kabat-Zinn, I discovered a local Buddhist meditation center and started attending sessions. The monks began chanting, and I was expected to chant along. Then there was silence. We practiced nothing except focusing on one thing only: our breath. That was a good thing, since up to that point, my constant anxiety and worry about myself and those I loved took my breath away. The usual, constant mental chatter in my brain was there as usual, but I'd sneak around it by bringing my focus back to my breath. I read some of the work of Tara Brach and practiced non-judgmentally diverting my thoughts away from catastrophic thinking.

After all, this was a new and pretty cool experience. Gaining momentum, I tried out a different, welcoming Buddhist temple. The chanting began. But this time, it was different chanting. Phonemes combined in intricate rhythms I had never heard before. They were compelling, like music to my ears. The chanting, made of brief, punctuated sound blasts, brought my focus to the immediate here and now. I began to feel a sense of calm and peacefulness wash through me. One could say I felt something moving in my spirit. But wait. What's this? I wasn't a spiritual person, I had decided long ago. "Stay open," I'd remind myself. "Healing is a journey, not an event. Trust the process."

Vocalizing monosyllabic vowels or "sound bites" became a peaceful, meditative experience. Breathing in and out calmed me and forced me to stay in the moment. The more I concentrated, the more empowered and better I felt. Once I learned about meditation and deep breathing, I hungered for more coping tools I knew I could rely on. I learned from Pema Chodron's work on mindfulness and suffering that healing is a continual, not linear process. I would have to keep developing and utilizing new coping skills, and meditation would become a daily practice for me.

Meditation and chanting led me to the next set of spiritually uplifting "sound bites." I turned to the practice of concentrating on "affirmations," which are indisputable declarations and facts about people, places, and things that stir the soul. Reading affirmations to oneself, or speaking them aloud, became equivalent to tasting a spoonful of sugar, a new type of medicine that made me feel better every time.

There are many free, wonderful websites that provide motivational "daily affirmations." I am a strong proponent of their benefit as they provide me with spiritual comfort and knowledge. So far, they also seem to help keep the cancer doctor away. Although I've listed a number of different Daily Affirmations websites in the References and Resources section of this memoir, I want to point out one of my favorite websites that I stumbled upon in my reading and research.

Ponder over some of the titles of the following *Daily Affirmations* sponsored by an online site called *Grief Connections and Schoedinger Funeral & Cremation Services:* I chose several meaningful ones (titles alone) and have presented them in random order. Do they provide the same instantaneous, knee-jerk reactions for you as they do for me?

Embracing Trust. Walking Away the Sorrows. Healing and Food. Going Within. Naturally Diminishing Grief. Are You Angry? Do Not Sit in Isolation. Unfinished Business. Recognize the Journey. New Life.

Humor

A PATIENT WITH a life-threatening illness often feels lonely, scared, and disconnected from the rest of humanity. Bridging that gap between loneliness and togetherness can be easily accomplished with a joke, or a pun, or riddle. When we laugh, we remember we're not completely alone. We're connected by a smile and our shared human need for happiness. The popular comedian, Woody Allen, when asked about his thoughts on mortality quipped, "I'm not afraid of death; I just don't want to be there when it happens."

In the wonderful old film, *Singin' in the Rain*, as Gene Kelly gleefully dances, he cries out from the bottom of his soul, "Make 'em laugh, make 'em laugh, make 'em laugh!" His dancing, singing, and clowning around tickles our funny-bone and makes us want to sing and dance and laugh out loud, too. Ever notice when someone in a room starts to yawn, then you do, too? Laughter is a lot like that. My old grandmother, a Russian Jewish immigrant with a thick Yiddish accent, used to say to me when I was a little girl, "Laugh and the whole world laughs with you. Cry and you cry alone."

Find what makes you laugh. It's a great grief escape. Could it be an old black and white slapstick film with Charlie Chaplin? Or maybe there's a TV show that would tickle your funny bone. Everyone loves to laugh. It's fun and it's free. Babies giggle long before they learn to talk and walk. But there's a more important biological reason why laughter is often a great way to help people cope with a life-threatening illness. It's been demonstrated scientifically that when a person starts to laugh, their hormone composition changes and reduces detrimental stress on the mind and body.

While fighting depression and locked in a mental ward, watching my favorite hilarious film, *Meet the Parents*, with Ben Stiller and a cast of comedic characters, was a great antidote to depression and stress. Watching that movie, every single day, helped me escape feeling miserable. Laughter distracted me from the miserable side-effects of the numerous medications my doctors prescribed. I was profoundly depressed, terrified and lonely, and I couldn't stop crying, but I was surprised to learn I could laugh. It became automatic the more I practiced concentrating on its pleasant sound. I couldn't feel anxious or depressed and laugh at the same time. I started to relax and my mood cheered up. If I could learn to laugh, that means there's hope for others, too.

Bernie Siegel, MD, an expert in the field of cancer treatment and holistic medicine, reminds us that we've got nothing to lose and everything to gain by maintaining hope. No one can predict what the future will bring. After all, despite what the cancer doctor initially told me that I would die without a bone marrow transplant, I'm still very much alive. If I could go back to the time of my illness, I would try to remind myself what Dr. Siegel teaches us, that is "hope is free."

Post-Traumatic Growth

HOW COULD I make sense of the three-year physical, mental, and emotional tribulation I somehow managed to survive? What were the turning points from illness to wellness? I look back and see how they actually began as seeds, planted during sessions with my psychotherapist, that germinated later on, outside her office walls. Turning points, or special "Ah-ha!" moments are hard to detail. It's not as though I can reflect back and recount each lesson as a distinct pearl, for there were so many countless moments in between each learning experience. In the end, each defining moment strings together like a gleaming necklace, a metaphor for the indescribable process of transformation itself.

Now that these tragedies occurred and I survived, how could I incorporate all that I had experienced into my life to help create a "new normal"? Suzanne Baer, PhD in Human Development and Aging from Fielding Graduate University, writes, "We are all life-long learners. Each of us is the creator and re-creator of our own lives." Moreover, how could I make sense of these experiences, and use what I learned along the way to help others who are now facing what I went through?

With time, I learned how my whole family was also affected by my experience of facing a life-threatening illness. Our family was swept up in a tornado to a far-away land, like Dorothy in *The Wizard of Oz*. This new landscape was completely unfamiliar and frightening. It shook our family foundation, and it rocked our sense of security, confidence, and the belief that we are in control of our destiny. We missed the familiarity, safety, and comfort of our old lives back on earth, and we yearned to find our way back home some way, somehow. There was no turning back, only forward, one small step at a time. Who could help us find our way out of this strange land? We looked everywhere to find resources that would point us in the right direction, and we encountered incredibly supportive friends, family, and total strangers along the way who wanted to walk alongside us, so we wouldn't be alone on our journey.

Just as important as it was for me to find the support I needed, our family members, friends and other caregivers needed to find healthy ways to manage their grief and loss, too. We struggled as best we could to research the support services that were available, but at that period of time when I was diagnosed and treated for leukemia and depression beginning in the year 1999, hospital and community-based support groups, especially for young children, were limited. Fortunately, that is not the case now, especially at forward-thinking, well-funded, state-of-the-art cancer teaching hospitals such as City of Hope National Medical Center, Dana Farber Cancer Institute, Johns Hopkins Medical Center, MD Anderson Cancer Center, and Memorial Sloan Kettering Cancer Center, to name a few. There is now emerging literature on guiding children through grief, including the leading work of Mary Ann and James P. Emswiler, founders of the New England Center for Loss & Transition and The Cove, along with Renee A. McIntyre, LCSW.

When a sudden, unexpected diagnosis of cancer or other chronic condition appears out of nowhere, the time and attention involved in combating the disease takes front and center. Suddenly, energy must be channeled into survival, and all other stresses seem less significant and must be put on the back burner. And yet, the previous, often unresolved stressors and problems don't just disappear. They co-exist. Stress plus stress equals more stress.

There was a strain on my marriage to begin with, and then it was tested in ways my husband and I couldn't possibly imagine. Conflict intensified for many different reasons and on many levels. The life of a cancer doctor is both exciting and demanding. People never stop getting cancer, and endurance is a necessity. For physicians, nurses, social workers, and other members of the medical team, the work hours are long, hospital policies have become increasingly burdensome, and patients can be quite demanding. Patience runs thin.

Winston Churchill famously said, "If you're going through hell, keep going." Ken and I were going through hell at the time, and that's just what we did. We had no choice. There were so many times we wanted to stop and give up. But because of our iron-clad commitment to stay married and keep the family together, we refused to give up until we could find a survival plan that would work for both of us. Thankfully, we had the funds and fortitude to seek professional counseling, and during that hard time, we went individually and together. We cried and yelled, but we listened to each other and worked as a team until we got through to the other side.

Surviving one life-changing catastrophe after another, first cancer and then depression, ultimately shaped our relationship in a positive way. We lived through a hurricane together, and we not only survived, but our bond was strengthened in a way we never expected. And since that time, my husband and I then had a turn to worry about his own life-threatening experience, during which he required emergency heart surgery where his life hung in the balance. Our shared afflictions made us stronger. As a family, we have matured and collectively grown together. Although there were many times Ken and our children were afraid they might lose their mother, they lived to see a much stronger mother emerge, one who was much more confident, understanding, and compassionate.

Once I could put my hospital treatments behind me, time passed and I could begin to see a future ahead. Then all I had left to do was figure out what to do next, and how and when. What was left was the task of repairing broken or disfigured relationships, getting back into physical shape, and dealing with the multitude of lingering medication side-effects, such as weight gain, dry skin, bone pain, and neuropathy. That was just the physical part. The mental and emotional recovery was just as difficult, if not more.

Once my depression lifted, I tried to get back to the things I used to love doing, like spending time with family and friends, boating, swimming, singing, and playing guitar. I also tried to stay open to adventuring down new roads as well. If you had told me I would ever have a green thumb, I wouldn't have believed you. Before cancer and depression, I was the last person you would want to ask to take care of your plants, for fear you'd return home from a vacation to a horticultural disaster. Years after my depression, I found myself with gardening gloves on, kneeling in the grass, planting my very first geranium. That began my next foray into making homemade, healthy vegetable soups, and creating multi-layer ice cream cakes, something not only I enjoyed, but family and friends did, too.

I learned to practice setting small, realistic goals, and still do, to prevent feeling overwhelmed. *Slow and steady wins the race*, I'd often remind myself. If I accidentally set my goals too high, I'd remind myself to break them into smaller, manageable parts. There were times I'd come home from a hospital stay and couldn't bear how messy and disorganized things had become around the house. It felt as if someone had shuffled a deck of wild playing cards that went flying through the house in all directions. Pots and pans, and articles of children's clothing, to name a few things, were mixed up and in the wrong places. Important phone numbers, address books, bank statements, bills, and medical or other insurance papers were also nowhere to be found.

My home had become unrecognizable. Living with what felt like a giant mess, internally and externally, stressed me out. I felt I would need to solve it *in a big way*. Trying to restore order after such disorder felt impossible. I'd wake up sweating. The anxiety would rise in my chest. "This job is too big. It'll take me days to put everything back in order." My heart would beat faster. I'd start to cry. And then, I straightened myself up and asked if there was another, more simple way to meet my objective. Could I somehow break down the great big goal

POST-TRAUMATIC GROWTH

of putting the whole house back together into smaller, manageable steps? Could I make a list of long-term and short-term goals so I'd have the benefit of seeing my progress in action? I wrote down and accomplished my first task: find my address book.

The "new me" discovered that I didn't need to be in control every moment. By tackling one short-term goal at a time, I was ultimately able to reach my long-term goal of getting my house of cards back together. I learned that it was okay not to have every part of my life in order. In fact, it became liberating to learn to live with a bit more mess and disorder. Now years later, my husband, Ken, will come home from work, take one look around and say, "How can you live this way? This house is a mess!" Breaking large goals into smaller goals as a coping tool for stress really works.

After feeling more on top of my own stress, my next step was to begin volunteering at the local elementary school to help children with special needs. It had been a great source of joy in the past to help youngsters develop reading and language skills, and I suspected that helping others could be a salve for my wounds. Returning to work, part-time at first, helped steadily build my confidence. Feeling rusty and out of practice, I knew I needed patience and perseverance in order to keep moving forward. After all, it was odd to be back in the driver's seat. I had been so sick for so long and had needed so much care. It had been quite a while since I felt I had something to give.

Once I was started feeling a bit like my old self again, it gave me hope for the future, as well as faith in the long process of healing grief. I was grateful to the many cheerleaders along the sidelines—friends, family, neighbors, and colleagues—who gave me the opportunity to demonstrate that I could be leaned on again and wouldn't fall apart. That required building trust between us again, a challenging but necessary part of the process. Working through grief helped me overcome my own suffering. I was ultimately able to transcend my grief and develop new goals that didn't seem possible before. Instead of turning away from my fears and worries about confronting death, I practiced accepting them, even "making friends with grief," regarding it like a familiar, old friend.

Trusting the process ultimately led me to a brand new place of insight and enabled me to appreciate a renewed outlook and gratitude for life and living. Through integrating my experiences and all that I learned, I had the good fortune of developing a new and different perspective. That all-knowing, well-meaning cancer survivor was right, when he whispered to me, "You'll see...you'll be glad one day. Cancer is a gift. It will change your life for the better." I was furious at the time, because I thought it was an insensitive comment, and that he was trying to sugar-coat the catastrophe I was facing. Didn't he know I liked my life exactly as it was, and that I didn't want my life to change?

My illnesses provided me with an incomparable learning opportunity to resolve my own grief and then have the privilege to help others do the same. Like Elisabeth Kübler-Ross, MD describes, our life challenges throw us through a tumbler and toss us around until we emerge polished, gleaming like diamonds, or with rough edges, depending on our perspective. She suggests that we should welcome the challenging "windstorms" of our lives, as they test our fortitude, teach us lessons about ourselves that strengthen us, and become a catalyst for personal growth and wisdom. Similarly, Joan Borysenko, PhD, writes about the process of transforming "wounds into wisdom." In their new book about "supersurvivors," authors David Feldman, PhD, and Lee Daniel Kravetz write about the link between suffering and success, as well as the transformation of trauma in the lives of ordinary people. They study the art of resiliency, and how an overwhelming crisis can open the door to post-traumatic growth.

Ongoing trauma and resiliency research, as well as my own personal experience, help underscore how even the greatest mental and physical suffering can be transformative, not only for the "identified patient" but for family members, friends, colleagues, and the community. The experiences I miraculously survived left me with more than a silver lining. Getting through this dreadful period in my life, moment by moment, became the first step toward a resolution of that difficult, painful time. Step by step, this journey helped me develop a broader outlook on life, exemplifying how setbacks can be the basis for personal growth and development of one's character.

Internationally renowned psychiatrist Victor Frankl, MD, PhD, a Holocaust survivor, writes about how we have the power to change our response to the traumatic events in our lives. Survivors can overcome obstacles and grow if they are able to find existential meaning. Nietzche said, "That which doesn't kill us makes us stronger." Cracking the code, and deciphering the existential meaning to my horrific journey became the key to thriving, not just surviving. I knew if I could make sense of what happened in my life, why it happened, and how it happened, it could hopefully have a positive, transformative impact on my life. After the suffering I endured and miraculous recovery I made, each day feels like a birthday, a fresh start. Every minute of every day, I know how lucky I am and how incredible it is that I got through what I did.

Making Friends With Grief

I LEARNED THAT grief, the set of complicated feelings associated with catastrophic loss, is normal, not pathological. There is loss of personal faith and identity, loss of the former healthy self, and loss or change in social relationships. Each person has a different set of circumstances that they bring to their cancer experience. Preconceived notions of how people typically handle a terminal illness can be disregarded, for there is no typical, nor right or wrong way to manage the complicated dimensions of grief. There is no one-size-fits-all. People who are suffering often ask, "When will I get over this?" There is no timetable. It takes as long as it takes. The experience of healing grief varies for each person, and that is the reason why people must find their own way to cope.

The most important part of the healing process or grief journey is to acknowledge and express these feelings of loss. Getting feelings out can help prevent depression and PTSD. Telling one's story over and over again diffuses its intensity and promotes healing. This important goal can be achieved in a variety of ways, with different strategies that feel comfortable and right for each individual.

When I was experiencing my own illnesses, I wished for the certainty that I'd feel better one day and that I'd soon get over feeling sad, frustrated, and hopeless. If there was only a guarantee. But grief doesn't work that way, and no matter how hard I tried, I couldn't simply "get over it." There wasn't a distinct beginning, middle or end. Healing was not an event or an action I could simply take. It was an arduous, unsteady course with stops and starts along the way. Two steps forward, three steps back.

Like ocean waves and the change of tides, the intensity of grief feelings would come and go. On some days, or even moments throughout each day, feelings would come crashing to shore. On other days, waves of grief would recede. I was sure I would never feel better, and yet, those brief moments gave me a glimmer of hope that life wouldn't always feel so hard. The only thing I learned to be certain of was uncertainty itself.

It took a long time to be less harsh and judgmental of myself for not getting better more quickly. The mental chatter would reel through my mind. "Why is this taking so long? When will I feel better? No one else has felt this bad for so long." With my negativity and tendency to feel like each and every decision or set back was catastrophic, I had become my own worst enemy. It was a struggle to practice being patient and to give into the notion that grief would need to take its own course, go at its own pace, and take as long as it would take. The best I could do was to be a witness of this process.

When those waves came crashing in, I needed to remind myself not to let my anxiety get the best of me. I practiced not panicking or judging myself, but simply sitting back and noticing and observing my worrisome feelings come and go. I needed to learn to trust that the process would be laborious—step by step, moment by moment—and to stick with it until it resolved itself naturally. This meant reminding myself every day, throughout each day, that worry was a wasted emotion, and that my energy would be better spent on finding ways to get through whatever it was that was on my plate.

Eventually, my perspective began to shift. Instead of constantly looking back, and wondering how soon I'd get back to my old self again, I practiced looking forward and staying on the lookout for tools to integrate feelings of grief and loss. As in nature, seasons continually change. Birth and new life move toward maturity, and ultimately, death. Like new spring buds that begin to blossom after the cold winter months pass, personal growth and transformation bloom for individuals who surrender to the pain of suffering.

An instrumental part of my recovery and renewal was learning how to turn my own unbearable suffering into a greater good. Healing my grief gave me the opportunity to develop into a more compassionate person, and to use my experience of loss to improve others' lives. I'm amazed when I look back on my journal entry after meeting my grief companion for the very first time. Although I knew how necessary the role was, it seemed unimaginable at that time that anyone could have enough inner strength to become a grief counselor. And here I was toward the end of my journey, with a brand-new conviction that this was a job I knew I must do. This transformation helped me know for sure that, in the face of disaster, the process of healing grief can happen, and eventually, life can take on a new normal.

Here is an entry from my journal, written after that very first painful session with my psychotherapist when I did nothing but cry:

The way I see it, I can't think of anything more important than having a dedicated grief companion. A grief companion belongs on every cancer unit and should be provided for anyone facing trauma or significant loss. I wish I had met mine the moment I found out that I had a life-threatening illness but was too scared to talk about it. But let's be honest. Who could have the strength to carry out that role? What a difficult job it must be. Sitting quietly and calmly, while suspending all judgment, my grief companion watches me cry uncontrollably, spilling out rage and sorrow. Who knows, maybe I'll become a grief counselor for children one day, if I'm lucky enough to make it through?

But God knows, who would want to be a grief counselor? Who could possibly handle it? How hard it must be to simply be with a patient in pain like that, serving as a receptacle or container for their pain and grief. It seems like it would be one of the most difficult jobs in the world to be able to provide unconditional compassion and empathy. I bet only Mother Teresa could manage to do a job like that.

The work of helping those with such intensity of despair seems so noble. Although the job to help others in despair seems incredibly difficult, I wonder if it could be rewarding on some level. The work seems sacred in a way, and it is a job that needs to be done. Maybe I could imagine after all that the gratification and personal reward of helping someone in this level of distress could be a great privilege. One day, I would like to try to make this dream a reality.

When I was at the height of my cancer treatments, I had an epiphany. As I described earlier, death drew near toward the end of the third cycle of inpatient treatments, and the moment arrived when I was about to die. I felt a very strange, warm, calming sensation enveloping my whole being from head to toe. Although I had read about near-death experiences, it was something unbelievable to me, and I certainly had never experienced anything like that in my lifetime.

With a mysterious high fever raging through my body, it was at that precise, singular second that an "Ah-ha" moment appeared before my eyes. I actually saw the white light I'd heard people describe. I firmly promised myself that if I lived, I would learn to become a grief counselor for children facing death, trauma, or fear of losing a loved one, a vital service that was unavailable to my own young children.

I was inspired to become a grief counselor by the work of Richard Tedeschi, PhD and others on "post-traumatic growth" and by my own frustration at becoming depressed without the support of a trained grief companion or counselor from the moment of diagnosis. Like Allen Wolfelt, PhD describes, it is important for those experiencing trauma and loss to be "companioned," not led or pulled. An instrumental part of the healing process was figuring out ways that I could transcend loss by transforming something that felt unbearable into an opportunity for growth. Healing can transcend grief and a new self can emerge, one who is dedicated to assisting others manage similar traumas.

Not only did trusting the process lead me to a brand new place of insight, but it led me to a new career that I love and have enjoyed for over ten years. Since overcoming two separate cancers and a deep depression, I have had the pleasure of volunteering as a grief support group facilitator for children and families. I have facilitated

◂ HEALING GRIEF

groups in schools and summer camps, as well as in hospitals as far away as Uganda and Ethiopia where my husband, Ken, and I travel to help others who may be facing life-threatening illnesses, or who may dealing with bereavement after a death. It is difficult to explain the redemptive qualities of grief counseling in words, other than to say it feels like a gift to now be able to companion others in deep grief who are facing their own difficult, spiritual journeys. More than hard work, supporting the bereaved is "heartwork."

Now, I am able to help others through their grief. They hope that I will be with them and walk beside them, not lead them down one path or another, but rather, accompany them on their chosen path. I know from experience how rocky a path that can be, and how arduous the climb, and that they will encounter twists and turns and lose their place along the way. From personal experience, I know I should not try to point them in the right direction, because there is no right or wrong way. Each person facing grief and loss must find his or her own way through.

"How can I thank you enough for all you've done?" I am asked by many people whose lives I've touched through my work. I tell them what I want them to know and understand, and that is, "I'm in awe of your journey and the hard times you are going though. It's an honor and privilege to serve as your grief companion."

A Special Note from Joan's Psychotherapist

A COLLEAGUE APPROACHED me about Joan and wondered if I had space to take her on as a client. For me, this request came at a time that I had room for a new client who needed intensive treatment. Taking Joan on turned out to be a good fortune not only for her, but also for me.

Early on in our work, Joan expressed the wish that I had known her before she had slid into severe depression. Yet the fingerprints of who Joan was, without the thief of depression (which robbed her of her vitality and creativity), were visible despite her dull, depressed eyes. I only needed to hear her talk about her kids, or listen to what Ken had to say about her, or take one look at the book she co-authored to have a sense of her essence which shone through even when she was entirely in the grip of an anxious depression.

We started out seeing each other twice a week, sitting together with Joan's intense despair. In the first phase of our work, I told her over and over that eventually the meds would kick in and do their job, which would then make our job of psychotherapy easier. But first I needed to hold her hand (metaphorically) and tell her I would see her through and out of this deep dark place. In the absence of her hope, I had to be the one who held the hope for her.

At times this was easy: from the start, Joan seemed responsive to my voice and my questions and suggestions. As agitated as I might find her in the waiting room, once in my office Joan usually calmed down. Other days, I myself worried that she would not get beyond her despair. On those days I reminded myself that things don't ever stay the same: the sun rises, the sun sets, and the light changes throughout the day. On those days, I also drew hope from another client who I was seeing at the time. The client was a young adult whose mom had been hospitalized for depression when he was a teenager. It had been a long haul, but he told me that he finally had his mom back. On those days, I also turned to my consultant who told me to keep putting one foot in front of the other and who reminded me that the going would be slow at first.

When Joan was without hope, it was my job to throw her a lifeline. That lifeline took different forms at different times. I told her that, while I had no idea how the process would unfold, I had faith in the process. I had seen it time and again and I had no reason to believe the contrary in her case. I also told her I had no business seeing her if I did not believe she could get well. Other times, I simply reminded her I would see her through this nightmare.

But maybe the most important lifeline I threw out was during her second hospitalization when I called her every evening. Some days she would talk and some days she would say that just keeping the receiver to her ear was more than she could bear. But regardless of how she responded to my calls, I wanted her to know I deeply cared, and I wanted her to carry my voice with her. I provided constancy while in her inner world, Joan was constantly falling apart.

It took courage on both our parts, but especially on Joan's part, to sit with her fears and pain. And courage she had! Over time, she launched into the next layers of fear, shame, self-doubt, sadness and trauma (from the leukemia treatments) as soon as she sat down. At times, she would sit down and begin reading from her journal, as writing was easier for her than speaking. Sometimes the unspeakable is easier to commit to paper before sharing with another person.

The hard work paid off; three years later Joan was flourishing again. And when a few years after we had stopped sitting together I

A SPECIAL NOTE FROM JOAN'S PSYCHOTHERAPIST

myself had a major medical event, followed by an anxious depression, I frequently drew strength from our work, thinking: if Joan could do it with my help I should be able to do it too with the help of a caring therapist.

Photographs of the Journey

Joan age 23, Ken age 25. The age of innocence.
Setting out on our life journey together.

Our family before cancer & depression: Joan, age 38,
Ken age 40, Cara age 12, Julie age 8, Kim age 4.

PHOTOGRAPHS OF THE JOURNEY

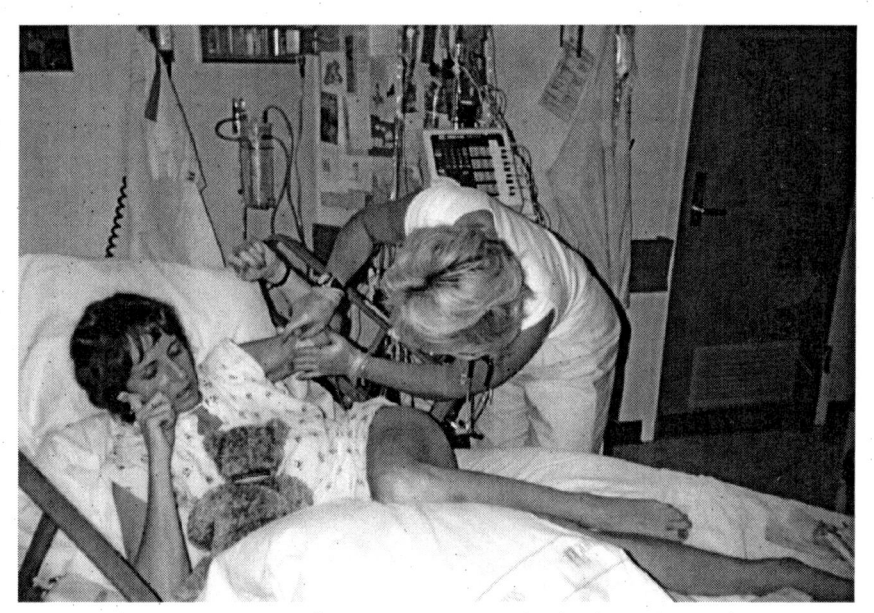

Wearing one of my many wigs. The highest dose of
morphine could not curb the leukemia bone pain.

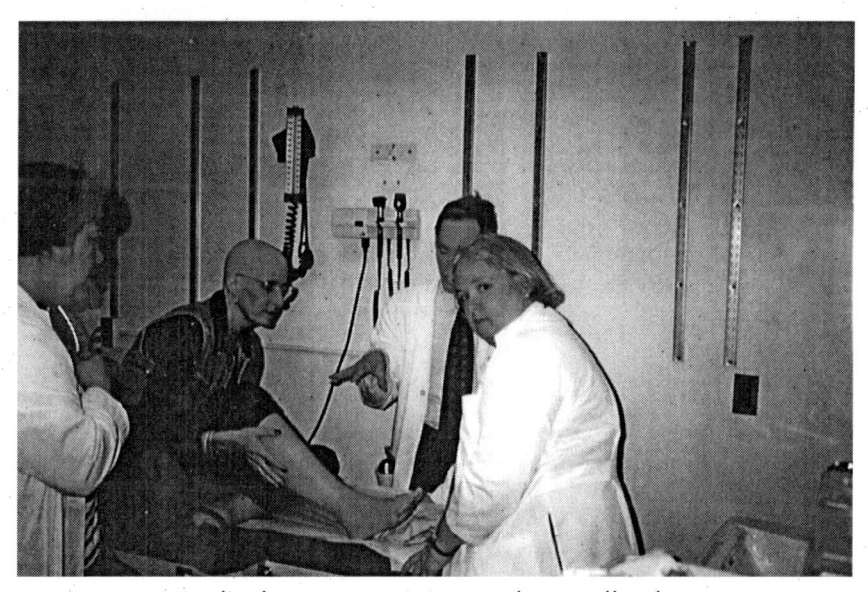

Medical team examining tender, swollen leg,
a side effect of chemotherapy.
High dose steroids were administered since antibiotics didn't help.

◄ **HEALING GRIEF**

Leaving the hospital with walker after inpatient chemotherapy treatment. Unable to bear weight from chemotherapy side effects. Mask required to prevent catching others' germs.

Celebrating completion of a 5-week inpatient cycle of chemotherapy. Wearing my bald head like a proud eagle.

PHOTOGRAPHS OF THE JOURNEY

Joan, age 40, Kimberly, age 6. Thrilled to have survived another inpatient cycle of chemotherapy.

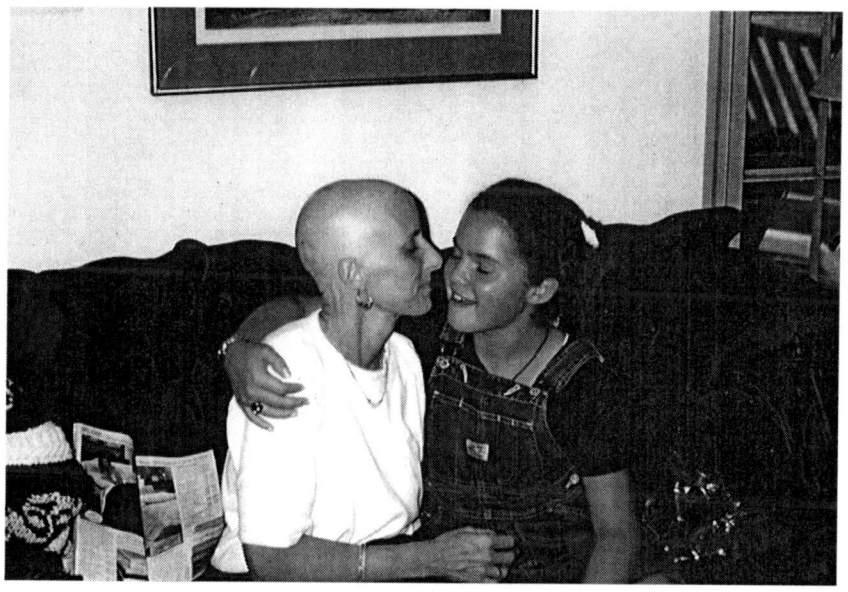

"I hope I'll be alive to watch you grow up."

◄ HEALING GRIEF

Joan home to revive red blood cell count in between treatment cycles. "I might die, but I still want to be a good mom."

My mom, Jane, at age 65 kissing my bald head, elated her daughter is still alive.

PHOTOGRAPHS OF THE JOURNEY

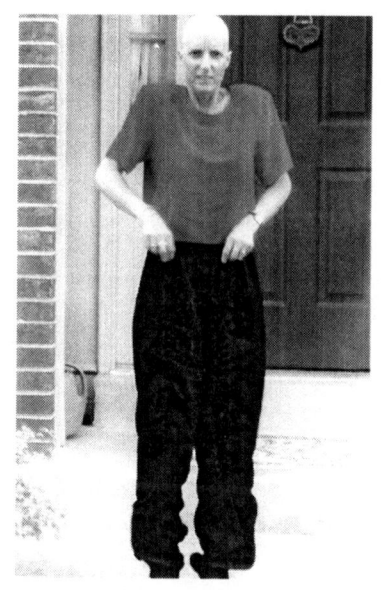

After another round of chemotherapy and twenty-five pound weight loss, looking like a concentration camp victim but relieved to have made it through alive.

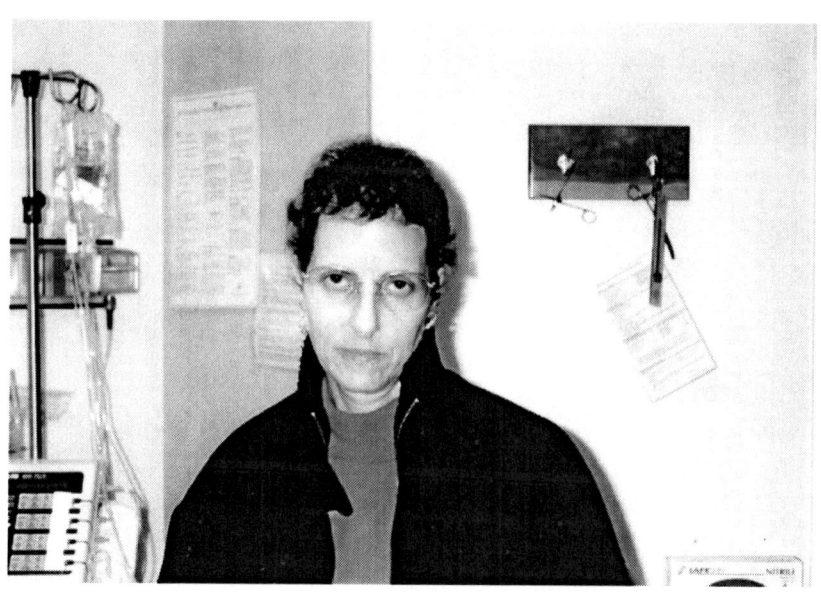

Lowest moment of all time. Worn down. Miserably depressed. Begging not to do one more cycle of inpatient treatments. I had had enough.

◄ **HEALING GRIEF**

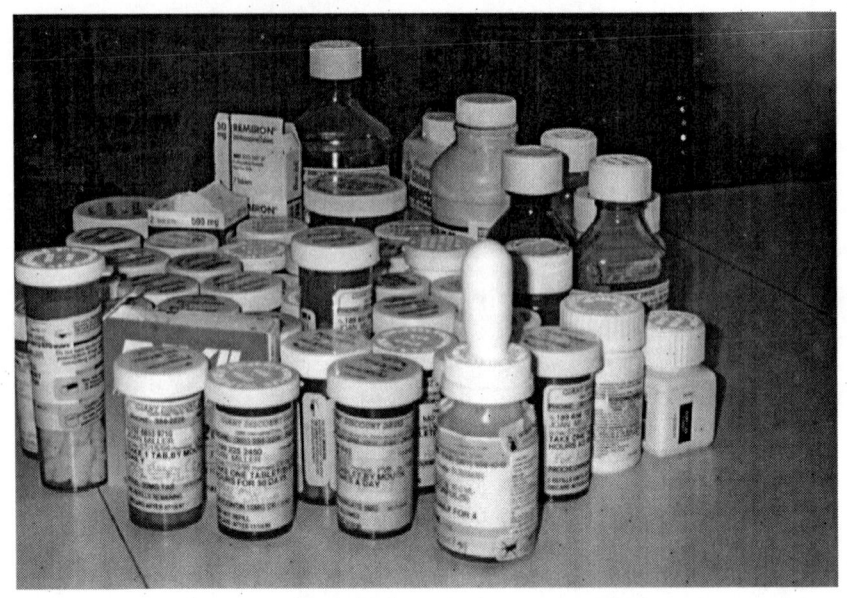

I had never taken any meds before cancer treatments, and now, this.

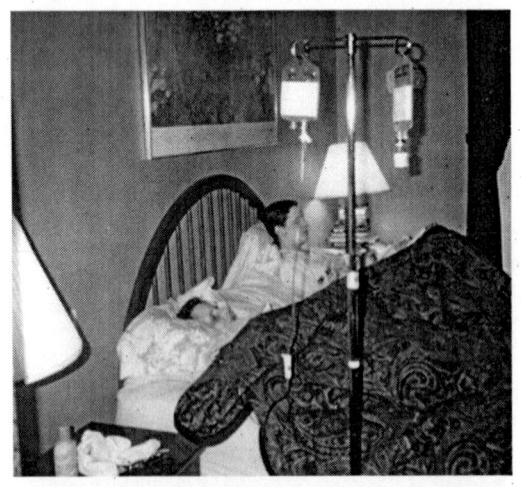

Lying in bed, downtrodden. Cara reading while keeping me company. Trying to help keep my spirits up.

PHOTOGRAPHS OF THE JOURNEY

Our family surviving and thriving together
ten years after cancer and depression.

With my dad and brothers, celebrating life.

◄ **HEALING GRIEF**

Ten years later, teaching journaling as a coping
strategy to a children's grief group at Uganda Hospice.

Enjoying injera and doro wat after a day's work at
Tikur Anbessa hospital cancer ward in Addis Ababa, Ethiopia.

References and Resources

Cancer Treatment

Cancer Support Community
  www.cancersupportcommunity.org

Cancer Wellness Center
  www.cancerwellness.org

Center for Mind Body Medicine
  http://cmbm.org/

City of Hope National Medical Comprehensive Cancer Center
  http://www.cityofhope.org/

Dana Farber Cancer Institute
  http://www.dana-farber.org/

Holland, Jimmie C., and Sheldon Lewis. *The Human Side of Cancer: Living with Hope, Coping with Uncertainty.* New York: Quill, 2001.

Holland, Jimmie C. *Psycho-Oncology.* Third ed. Oxford: Oxford University Press, 2015.

Gordon, James S. *Manifesto for a New Medicine: Your Guide to Healing Partnerships and the Wise Use of Alternative Therapies.* Reading, MA: Addison-Wesley, 1997.

LeShan, Lawrence L. *Cancer as a Turning Point: A Handbook for*

HEALING GRIEF

People with Cancer, Their Families, and Health Professionals. Rev. ed. New York: Plume, 1994.

Marlene and Stewart Greenebaum Cancer Center at University of Maryland Medical Center
http://umm.edu/programs/cancer

MD Anderson Cancer Center
http://www.mdanderson.org/

Memorial Sloan Kettering Cancer Center
https://www.mskcc.org/

Miller, Kenneth D. *Choices in Breast Cancer Treatment: Medical Specialists and Cancer Survivors Tell You What You Need to Know.* Baltimore, MD: Johns Hopkins University Press, 2008.

Miller, Kenneth D. *Excellent Care for Cancer Survivors: a Guide to Fully Meet Their Needs in Medical Offices and in the Community.* Santa Barbara, CA: Praeger, 2012.

Miller, Kenneth D. *Medical and Psychosocial Care of the Cancer Survivor.* Sudbury, MA: Jones and Bartlett Publishers, 2010. Chapter 5: S.L. Jim, PhD, Heather, and Paul Jacobsen, PhD. "Finding Benefits in the Cancer Experience: Post-Traumatic Growth."

Sidney Kimmel Comprehensive Center Cancer Center at Johns Hopkins

http://www.hopkinsmedicine.org/kimmel_cancer_center/

Siegel, Bernie S. *Love, Medicine & Miracles: Lessons Learned about Self-Healing from a Surgeon's Experience with Exceptional Patients.* New York: Harper Collins, 1998.

Susan G. Komen For the Cure
www.komen.org

Weil, Andrew. *Health and Healing: The Philosophy of Integrative Medicine.* Rev. ed. Boston: Houghton Mifflin, 2004.

Yale Cancer Center
http://www.yalecancercenter.org/

Cancer Support for Family Members

Emswiler, Mary Ann, and James P. Emswiler. *Guiding Your Child Through Grief.* New York: Bantam Books, 2000.

Harpham, Wendy Schlessel, and Jonas Kulikauskas. *When a Parent Has Cancer: A Guide to Caring for Your Children.* Rev. Ed., 1st Perennial Currents ed. New York: Perennial Currents, 2004.

Loscalzo, Matthew J., and Marc Heyison. *For the Women We Love: A Breast Cancer Action Plan and Caregiver's Guide for Men.* Baltimore, MD: Bartleby Press, 2007.

When Families Grieve. Sesame Workshop. http://www.sesameworkshop.org/what-we-do/our-initiatives/when-families-grieve/

Mental Illness: Bipolar, Depression, Post-Traumatic Stress, Suicide

DePaulo, J. Raymond, and Leslie Alan Horvitz. *Understanding Depression: What We Know and What You Can Do About It.* New York: Wiley, 2002.

Gordon, James S. *Unstuck: Your Guide to the Seven-stage Journey out of Depression.* New York: Penguin Press, 2008.

National Action Alliance for Suicide Prevention
http://actionallianceforsuicideprevention.org/

National Alliance on Mental Illness
https://www.nami.org/

National Suicide Prevention Lifeline
http://www.suicidepreventionlifeline.org/

Jamison, Kay R. *Exuberance: The Passion for Life.* New York: Vintage Books, 2005.

Jamison, Kay R. *Night Falls Fast: Understanding Suicide.* New York: Vintage Books, 2000.

Jamison, Kay Redfield. *Touched with Fire: Manic-depressive Illness and the Artistic Temperament.* New York: Free Press Paperbacks Published by Simon & Schuster, 1996.

Knaus, William J. *The Cognitive Behavioral Workbook for Depression: A Step-by-step Program.* 2nd ed. Oakland, CA: New Harbinger Publications, 2012.

Levine, Peter A. *Waking the Tiger: Healing Trauma.* Berkeley, CA: North Atlantic Books, 1997.

McBride, J. LeBron. *Spiritual Crisis: Surviving Trauma to the Soul.* New York: Haworth Pastoral Press, 1998.

McCann, I. Lisa. *Psychological Trauma and the Adult Survivor: Theory, Therapy, and Transformation.* New York: Brunner/Mazel, 1990.

Miklowitz, David Jay. *The Bipolar Disorder Survival Guide: What You and Your Family Need to Know.* 2nd ed. New York: Guilford Press, 2011.

Miller, Kenneth D. *Medical and Psychosocial Care of the Cancer Survivor.* Sudbury, MA: Jones and Bartlett Publishers, 2010. Chapter 4: Mitch Golant, PhD, and Megan Taylor-Ford. "Post-Traumatic Stress in Cancer Survivors."

Mondimore, Francis Mark. *Bipolar Disorder: A Guide for Patients and Families.* 2nd ed. Baltimore, MD: Johns Hopkins University Press, 2006.

Solomon, Andrew. *The Noonday Demon: An Atlas of Depression.* New York: Simon & Schuster, 2002.

Szasz, Thomas. *Coercion as Cure: A Critical History of Psychiatry.* New Brunswick, NJ: Transaction Publishers, 2009.

Szasz, Thomas. *The Myth of Mental Illness: Foundations of a Theory of Personal Conduct.* New York: Harper Perennial, 2010.

Van der Kolk, Bessel A. *The Body Keeps the Score: Brain, Mind, and Body in the Healing of Trauma.* New York: Viking Books, 2014.

WebMD Depression Center
http://www.webmd.com/depression/

Winell, MD, James, and Andrew J. Roth, MD. "Depression in Cancer Patients." Oncology Journal, 2004. http://www.cancernetwork.com/review-article/depression-cancer-patients.

Grief and Loss, Death and Dying

365 Daily Email Affirmations by Grief Connections and Schoedinger Funeral & Cremation Services
http://www.schoedinger.com/grief-and-healing/daily-email-affirmations

Byock, Ira. *Dying Well: Peace and Possibilities at the End of Life.* New York: Riverhead Books, 1998.

The Cove Center for Grieving Children
http://www.covect.org/

The Center for Grieving Children
http://grievingchildren.org/

The Grief Toolbox
http://thegrieftoolbox.com/

Hello Grief: A Place to Share and Learn About Grief and Loss
http://www.hellogrief.org

Hospice Caring, Inc.
http://www.hospicecaring.org/

Gilbert, Kei H. *From Grief to Memories.* Silver Spring, MD: Soras, 2001.

Lerner, Harriet Goldhor. *The Dance of Connection: How to Talk to Someone When You're Mad, Hurt, Scared, Frustrated, Insulted, Betrayed, or Desperate.* New York: Quill, 2002.

HEALING GRIEF

The Moyer Foundation
http://www.moyerfoundation.org/

National Alliance for Grieving Children
http://www.nationalallianceforgrievingchildren.org/

Pinkola Estés, Clarissa
http://www.clarissapinkolaestes.com/bio.htm

Terkel, Studs. *Will the Circle Be Unbroken?: Reflections on Death, Rebirth, and Hunger for a Faith*. New York: Ballantine Books, 2002.

Viorst, Judith. *Necessary Losses: The Loves, Illusions, Dependencies, and Impossible Expectations That All of Us Have to Give Up in Order to Grow*. New York: Fireside, 1998.

Welshons, John E. *Awakening from Grief: Finding the Way Back to Joy*. 2nd ed. Makawao, Maui, HI: Inner Ocean, 2003.

Wolfelt, Alan. *Companioning the Bereaved: A Soulful Guide for Caregivers*. Fort Collins, CO: Companion, 2006.

Memoirs

Allende, Isabel, and Margaret Sayers Peden. *Paula*. New York: Harper Perennial, 2008.

Armstrong, Lance, and Sally Jenkins. *It's Not About the Bike: My Journey Back to Life*. New York: Putnam, 2000.

Bartocci, Barbara. *From Hurting to Happy: Transforming Your Life after Loss*. Notre Dame, IN: Sorin Books, 2002.

Bauby, Jean. *The Diving Bell and the Butterfly*. New York: A.A. Knopf, 1997.

Berg, Elizabeth. *Talk before Sleep: A Novel*. New York: Random House, 1994.

REFERENCES AND RESOURCES

Campbell, Joseph, and Phil Cousineau. *The Hero's Journey: Joseph Campbell on His Life and Work*. 3rd ed. Novato, CA: New World Library, 2014.

Cox, Lynne. *Swimming to Antarctica: Tales of a Long-distance Swimmer*. Boston: Houghton Mifflin Harcourt, 2005.

Frank, Anne. *Anne Frank: The Diary of a Young Girl*. New York: Bantam Books, 1993.

Grandin, Temple. *Thinking in Pictures: And Other Reports from My Life with Autism*. 2nd Vintage Books ed. New York: Vintage Books, 2006.

Grealy, Lucy. *Autobiography of a Face*. New York: Perennial, 2003.

Hegi, Ursula. *Stones From the River*. New York: Simon & Schuster, 1995.

Henderson, Carol. *Losing Malcolm: A Mother's Journey through Grief*. Jackson, MS: University Press of Mississippi, 2001.

Jamison, Kay R. *An Unquiet Mind*. New York: Vintage Books, 1996.

Keller, Helen. *The Story of My Life*. Dover ed. Mineola, NY: Dover Publications, 1996.

Kübler-Ross, Elisabeth. *The Wheel of Life: A Memoir of Living and Dying*. New York: Touchstone, 1998.

MacPherson, Myra. *She Came to Live out Loud: An Inspiring Family Journey through Illness, Loss, and Grief*. New York: Scribner, 1999.

Masters, Peter. *Striking Back: A Jewish Commando's War against the Nazis*. Novato, CA: Presidio, 1997.

Monette, Paul. *Borrowed Time: An AIDS Memoir*. San Diego, CA: Harcourt Brace, 1998.

Nguyen, Kien. *The Unwanted: A Memoir of Childhood*. Boston: Back Bay Books, 2002.

HEALING GRIEF

Pelzer, Dave. *A Child Called It: One Child's Courage to Survive*. Deerfield Beach, FL: Health Communications, Inc., 1995.

Pipher, Mary Bray. *Letters to a Young Therapist: Stories of Hope and Healing*. Paperback ed. New York: Basic Books, 2005.

Price, Jill, and Bart Davis. *The Woman Who Can't Forget: The Extraordinary Story of Living with the Most Remarkable Memory Known to Science: A Memoir*. New York: Free Press, 2008.

Rapoport, Judith L. *The Boy Who Couldn't Stop Washing: The Experience & Treatment of Obsessive-Compulsive Disorder*. New York: Dutton, 1989.

Reeve, Christopher. *Nothing is Impossible: Reflections on a New Life*. New York: Random House, 2002.

Richman, Sophia. *A Wolf in the Attic: The Legacy of a Hidden Child of the Holocaust*. New York: Haworth Press, 2002.

Steele, Ken, and Claire Berman. *The Day the Voices Stopped: A Memoir of Madness and Hope*. New York: Basic Books, 2001.

Tillman, David. *In the Failing Light*. North Andover, MA: Essex Press, 1999.

Vujicic, Nick, and Kanae Vujicic. *Love Without Limits: A Remarkable Story of True Love Conquering All*. Colorado Springs, CO: WaterBrook Press, 2014.

Wise, Terry L. *Waking Up: Climbing through the Darkness*. Updated ed. Eau Claire, WI: Missing Peace, LLC, 2012.

Yalom, Irvin D. *Momma and the Meaning of Life: Tales of Psychotherapy*. New York: Perennial, 2000.

Mindfulness and Meditation

Armstrong, Karen. *Buddha*. New York: Lipper/Penguin, 2004.

Brach, Tara. *Radical Acceptance: Embracing Your Life with the Heart of a Buddha*. New York: Bantam Books, 2003.

REFERENCES AND RESOURCES

Brantley, Jeffrey, and Wendy Matik. *Daily Meditations for Calming Your Anxious Mind.* Oakland, CA: New Harbinger Publications, 2008.

Chernin, Kim. *A Different Kind of Listening: My Psychoanalysis and Its Shadow.* New York: Harper Collins Publishers, 1995.

Chodron, Pema. *When Things Fall Apart: Heart Advice for Difficult Times.* Boston: Shambhala Publications, 1998.

Epstein, Mark. *Going on Being: Buddhism and the Way of Change.* Trade Pbk. ed. New York: Broadway Books, 2002.

Epstein, Mark. *Going to Pieces without Falling Apart: A Buddhist Perspective on Wholeness.* New York: Broadway Books, 1998.

Kabat-Zinn, Jon. *Full Catastrophe Living: Using the Wisdom of Your Body and Mind to Face Stress, Pain, and Illness.* New York: Random House, 1990.

Kabat-Zinn, Jon. *Wherever You Go, There You Are: Mindfulness Meditation in Everyday Life.* New York: Hyperion, 1994.

Naparstek, Belleruth. *A Meditation to Help Ease Pain.* Akron, OH: Health Journeys, 1992.

Naparstek, Belleruth. *Staying Well with Guided Imagery.* New York: Warner Books, 1995.

Nix, Jackie, and Lucie Hall. *The Mindfulness Solution to Pain: Step-by-step Techniques for Chronic Pain Management.* Oakland, CA: New Harbinger, 2009.

Trungpa, Cho. *Shambhala: The Sacred Path of the Warrior.* New ed. Boston: Shambhala Publications, 2007.

Williams, Mark. *Freeing Yourself from Chronic Unhappiness: Guided Meditation Practices for the Mindful Way through Depression.* New York: Guilford Publications Inc, 2007.

◄ HEALING GRIEF

Journaling

Baldwin, Christina. *Life's Companion: Journal Writing as a Spiritual Quest*. New York: Bantam Books, 1991.

Foster, Patricia. *The Healing Circle: Authors Writing of Recovery*. New York: Plume Book, 1998.

Goldberg, Natalie. *Writing Down the Bones: Freeing the Writer Within*. 2nd ed. Boston: Shambhala Publications, 2005.

Metzger, Deena. *Writing for Your Life: A Guide and Companion to the Inner Worlds*. San Francisco, CA: Harper San Francisco, 1992.

Thomas, Frank P. *How to Write the Story of Your Life*. Cincinnati, OH: Writer's Digest Books, 1984.

Music for Healing Grief

Sand & Water by Beth Nielson Chapman

Wind Beneath My Wings by Bette Midler

Fire and Rain by James Taylor

The Circle Game by Joni Mitchell

The Prayer by Josh Groban

Post-Traumatic Growth

Barasch, Marc. *The Healing Path: A Soul Approach to Illness*. New York: Penguin Arkana, 1995.

Borysenko, Joan, and Larry Rothstein. *Minding the Body, Mending the Mind*. New York: Da Capo Lifelong, 2007.

Brehony, Kathleen A. *After the Darkest Hour: How Suffering Begins the Journey to Wisdom*. New York: Holt Paperbacks, 2000..

Feldman, David B., and Lee Daniel Kravetz. *Supersurvivors: The Surprising Link Between Suffering and Success.* New York: Harperwave, 2015.

Greenspan, Miriam. *Healing through the Dark Emotions: The Wisdom of Grief, Fear, and Despair.* Boston: Shambhala Publications, 2004.

Kushner, Harold S. *When Bad Things Happen to Good People.* New York: Anchor Books, 2004.

Tedeschi, R. G., and L.G. Calhoun. "Post-traumatic Growth: Conceptual foundations and empirical evidence." Psychological Inquiry, 2004. http://psycnet.apa.org/psycinfo/2004-11807-003

Wiesel, Elie, and Marion Wiesel. *The Night Trilogy: Night; Dawn; Day.* New York: Hill and Wang, 2008.

Spirituality and Hope & Healing

Barks, Coleman. *The Essential Rumi: New Expanded Edition.* New York: Harper Collins Publishers, 2004.

Fleck, G. Peter. *Come as You Are: Reflections on the Revelations of Everyday Life.* Boston: Beacon Press, 1993.

Lama, Dalai. *The Art of Happiness: A Handbook for Living.* 10th Anniversary Edition ed. New York: Riverhead Books, 2009.

Remen, Rachel Naomi. *Kitchen Table Wisdom: Stories That Heal.* 10th Anniversary ed. New York: Riverhead Books, 2006.

Welwood, John. *Toward a Psychology of Awakening: Buddhism, Psychotherapy, and the Path of Personal and Spiritual Transformation.* Boston: Shambhala Publications, 2002.

Wilber, Ken. *Grace and Grit: Spirituality and Healing in the Life and Death of Treya Killam Wilber.* 2nd ed. Boston: Shambhala Publications, 2000.

CPSIA information can be obtained at www.ICGtesting.com
Printed in the USA
BVOW04s0714121015

421904BV00001B/1/P

9 781478 760016